EFFECTIVE NETWORKING IN THE RELATIONSHIP AGE

Larry Klapow

Camp K
Marketing & Media

© 2009 By Larry Klapow, Camp K Marketing & Media

Published by Camp K Marketing & Media
86 Verissimo Dr., Novato, CA. 94947
(408) 710-0796
larry@renanetworks.com
First Printing September 2009

Printed in the United States of America

This publication is designed to provide accurate and relevant information in regard to the subject matter covered. It is sold with the understanding that neither the author nor publisher is engaged in rendering legal, accounting, tax or any other professional service. If legal or other expert assistance is required, the services of a competent professional person should be sought.

ISBN   978-0-9823441-0-1

Library of Congress Control Number (LCCN): 2009908687

IN MEMORY OF
LISA DIANE KLAPOW

SPECIAL THANKS TO:

BILL & SHANNON QUIGLEY
THE RIDDLE BROTHERS
LEAH REICH
DIANE SANGSTER

CONTENTS

TO BEGIN

*"Only a life lived for
others is a life worth while."*
~ Albert Einstein

It was late morning and we had just been deployed on another patrol mission over the Gulf of Oman. The year was 1986 and I was a U.S. Navy flight engineer, part of a 12-man crew responsible for flying oil escorts for U.S. tankers to ensure they made it safely out of hostile waters. I had been in the Navy for six years and had been through every type of emergency and torture training imaginable. Still, I will never forget the day our plane was going down.

I was seated in the cockpit of a Lockheed P-3 Orion, a long-range antisubmarine warfare aircraft used for patrols. Everything was going smoothly when suddenly one of the crew smelled smoke. A fire had broken out in the cockpit and unless we could find the source, we would have to abandon the plane. We put on oxygen masks and the crew immediately began the standard "fire of unknown origin" detection procedure. Adhering to a checklist, we sequentially shut down power to each system, hoping that one would cut off the source of the fire. We were having no luck.

Almost 15 minutes had gone by and we still had not found the source of the blaze. The smoke in the cockpit was getting heavier. As systems were powered off, the plane lost altitude.

The situation looked desperate. We sent emergency radio transmissions, announcing our intent to ditch the plane in the hope that our base or U.S. planes in the area would receive the message and pick us up if we made it. Landing a propeller plane on water is a violent undertaking and seldom leaves survivors. Still, all I could do was follow procedure and have faith in the crew to persist in their search for the cause of the fire.

Finally, the defining moment arrived when, just as we were about to abandon the aircraft, a crewmate's voice shouted that he had found the source of the fire – a black box inside a cabinet in the cockpit. Within seconds, we extinguished the fire, pulled the nose of the plane up and headed back to base.

When I think back to that time, I remember feeling this immense relief and overwhelming gratitude for my crew, on whom I had depended and who didn't let us down. Thanks to them, I walked away alive and with this lesson: Life is short and uncertain and people are the most valuable asset we have. Having positive relationships with people you can trust is the most important thing in life.

Overcoming adversity, achieving your goals and finding success all depend on relationships. Not on how smart you are or how much you know. Those things are helpful, but only to a point. When it comes to defining moments in life, the attainment of success depends most of all on the people in your life.

I learned this lesson in a plane over hostile territory in the Gulf and I have seen it time and time again. The stronger your networks of people are, the more opportunities you will encounter. The better your relationships are, the more likely your chances to succeed. It is as simple as that.

What is not so simple or, at least not as widely understood, is the "how" – how to attract the right people into your life and how to characterize your relationships with them in ways which will enable you to achieve your goals. That's what this book is about.

How do you find people who need and value what you offer? Whether you are looking for new business clients, individuals with expertise to help with a special project, or new friends to become part of your close personal network, finding the right people at the right time can be a difficult matter, which many find perplexing. Where are the right people when you need them? How can you find them? How can you communicate with them? How can you really connect?

This book will answer these questions. It will show you how to meet and form relationships with people for powerful results in business and in personal life. It will share secrets and insights that have proven successful in developing a highly effective network of contacts and it will outline a specific process, which will show you how to develop and maximize relationships with the people who can empower you to achieve your goals.

The World We Live In

Discovering the right people at the right time in your life and reaching them is no easy task. Consider the world we live in.

Each day, we are exposed to approximately 3,000 messages in one form or another. These messages range from television and newspaper advertisements to radio announcements, billboards and internet messages which crowd our landscape and compete for our attention, whether we like it or not. Logos are plastered everywhere. Retail stores and even gas stations, feature video monitors blaring programs, which grasp for a piece of our minds, making real peace of mind a rare and sought-after condition.

We live in an age of information overload and "always on" communication. Virtually everyone has access to tools that either didn't exist 20 years ago or were too costly for most. Today, we have cell phones, computers, email, faxes, instant messaging, Twitter and so much more.

It is no wonder our attention spans are getting shorter and our patience thinner. The average length of a television commercial has been cut to 30 seconds from one minute due to a mass lack of focus.

In an environment filled with so much noise, our society is responding with a phenomenon called "cocooning." It is a trend of retreating from the outside world and it is evident in a host of lifestyle changes:

- Living in gated communities
- Driving "into" garages and closing the door behind us
- Screening calls with caller I.D. and voice mail
- Using post office boxes for privacy and protection from identity theft
- Cameras and home security systems
- Do not call, do not fax and no spam lists
- Increase in home theaters vs. public theaters
- Online shopping versus retail stores
- Grocery and Prescription deliveries to the home, to name a few

In addition to communication overload and cocooning, the high cost of marketing makes it challenging to convey a clear message and attract customers.

Business marketing and advertising are becoming expensive propositions. Unless you have the financial resources of a Fortune 500 company, you will find it difficult to get your brands, goods or services into the minds of consumers.

Corporate America has spent billions in advertising. Most of us cannot even begin to compete at that level. The good news is we do not have to.

The Path to Success

My path to success was not without stumbling blocks. After I left the Navy and returned to civilian life, I felt isolated and inferior. I had no idea how I was going to make a living. Who would guess I would one day be president of one of the San Francisco Bay Area's largest real estate operations, overseeing 16 offices and a talented team of over 1,000 real estate professionals.

Looking back, I have no doubt I owe my tremendous success to one factor – effective networking. That's the first piece of good news.

The second piece of good news is that I am now going to share my process for building solid and long-lasting relationships.

You may think you already know about networking. You may wonder how this book differs from the multitude of other books on networking. Let me tell you.

First, this book presents a logical system you can follow – a seven-step process for developing and maximizing effective networks. A chapter is devoted to each step. You can read them sequentially or pick a chapter, one at a time, and focus on that step.

Second, this book is low on filler and high on actionable, factual, usable content, including proprietary principles you won't find elsewhere. The steps in this book work. I have lived and taught them as well as mentored others with great success. You can feel confident that if you apply these easy-to-follow steps and the principles they encompass, you will see results in a very short time.

Third, you will see how traditional networking practices and online social networking can complement each other and the role that each plays in helping you achieve your goals. This is not your grandfather's networking. The world is changing and so are the ways we interact with people. This book acknowledges these changes and examines the impact for businesses and individuals alike.

Finally, you will learn new ways to think about the people in your life and new ideas about relationships. As the book title states, we live in the **Relationship Age**. You will learn what that means and how concepts like "Social Capital" and adding value to your relationships can help you achieve your goals.

I have come a long way since my harrowing ride in the cockpit of that P-3 Orion over the Gulf of Oman. I have encountered good fortune and I have learned specific, reliable steps for achieving my goals. It is my delight to share them with you here.

Why you wonder would I want to share such precious secrets with others. You will discover why in the pages that follow. Read on and learn how to transform your own life.

Larry Klapow

THE NETWORKING SOLUTION

*"Up the proverbial creek? If you've got a network,
you've always got a paddle."*

~ Harvey Mackay

Networking. Just hearing the word makes some people cringe. It is perfectly understandable. The image the mind conjures up is a room full of people, each with a wad of business cards that they eagerly shove into one another's hands. Everyone wants one thing from the others in the room – new business. Attendees measure the success of the event by how many cards they walk away with.

The problem is, the concept of attending a networking event to obtain new leads is flawed by design. If everyone is there to tell their own story, who is listening to your story? If everyone is there to receive business, who is prepared to give you business?

The giving, the one thing most people do not even think about, is actually one of the secrets to networking success. It is integral to building a relationship.

Imagine a different scenario. You go to a networking event for one primary purpose – to meet and get to know new people to whom you can give something or help in some way. You don't rush through the room, meeting as many people as time allows. You don't give away your business cards to everyone you meet. You focus on meeting a few people and having a meaningful conversation with them, getting to know them and asking what you can do to help them. You ask for their business card.

Then, after the event, you follow up with a phone call or email. You send them something or tell them about something you think might be meaningful to them. You open the door to a relationship. You ask for nothing in return.

This is the start of effective networking. It is a paradigm shift. Most people define networking as the act of finding people fast to obtain something they need and, only secondarily, if at all, helping others do the same.

Wake-up call! The most effective networking is not about receiving, but about giving. It is a type of networking tailored to the times.

The Relationship Age

The world is entering a new era. The United States started out as an agrarian economy. We then moved to a manufacturing economy. Today, we are enjoying the benefits of a knowledge and information economy. Looking to the future, I believe there is a new revolution upon us and it is being driven by the consumer.

From the millions of people making use of social networking sites to the consumer demand for a larger say in how and what they buy, how governments are run and how business is transacted, people are shifting their priorities.

As countries around the world struggle with economic and political challenges, people are yearning for relationships and it looks like we are now entering what I call the Relationship Age. People worldwide seek more than material wealth and quick and superficial contacts. They want environmental consciousness and a depth of connection characterized by positive interactions.

Look around. The new forms of communication and new technologies developed during the Information Era are changing the game. Past frustrations with corporate performance, governments, education, health care, environmental policy and the economy are providing the motivation for a new mindset. A new age is fast approaching and it requires a new definition of networking.

Networking in the Relationship Age

In the Relationship Age, networking is defined as a method of building strategic alliances and mutually beneficial relationships for the betterment of BOTH parties. It is doing things for others with the expectation of gaining nothing in return.

This is a huge shift from the networking of the past where the focus was on connecting with people to conduct fast transactions. Now, the focus is on developing lasting alliances in which you will discover ways to help others.

To be successful, your goal should be to approach every situation you encounter and everyone you meet with the objective of adding value to his or her life.

Make it known to the members of your network you are interested in helping and serving them. Do this in all your conversations and correspondence, including email. With consistency, in a short time, your credibility will rise dramatically.

As an example, in every conversation, I end by saying to the other person, **"Please let me know if there is anything I can do for you."** My employees got so used to hearing this phrase , when I walked around the office to see how everyone was doing, before I had a chance to say anything, they would smile, hold up their hands and say, "Nothing today Larry. I am doing great!"

The consistency of my message had made it clear that they could trust me to be there for them, just as they were there for me - day in and day out. That is a Mutually Beneficial Relationship.

Developing a strong network in line with this new definition of networking does not come automatically. It requires a choice. There are two ways to meet people whom you may add to your network and, once you meet them, two ways to greet them. Meeting people can be serendipitous or strategic.

Serendipitous experiences are those chance encounters that occur when you bump into someone. Perhaps you are on a plane and you strike up a conversation with the person next to you. Without intent, you mention your line of work and it turns out, unexpectedly, your new acquaintance has a real need for what you do. These encounters happen randomly. They can be wonderful surprises, but may not be relied on as a method for developing a strong network of contacts.

Strategic meetings, on the other hand, are planned and on purpose. They are thought-out actions to add new contacts to your network and they are what we will focus on throughout our discussion of networking.

Whether your meetings with people are serendipitous or strategic, you are still faced with the choice of how to greet them. Will it be in accordance with the old definition of networking or with our new definition of "**Effective Networking In The Relationship Age?**"

Conditioned by the world around us where everyone else is shouting their messages, without intention, we have become almost programmed to start talking about ourselves, to tell our own story, to sell our own products, services and ideas.

If we are to be successful in fully making the paradigm shift from the old view to our new vision of networking, we will need to make a conscious decision to stop selling and start serving.

This requires us to recognize not only what networking is, but also what it is not.

What Networking Is Not

Here is what networking is not:

Networking is not marketing – trying to promote your products or services to others so they will be more inclined to purchase them.

Networking is not selling – convincing someone to purchase your products or services and completing the transaction.

Networking is not schmoozing – a term that can be offensive and refers to conversing with people in an insincere way.

The event described at the beginning of this chapter, where people went to find new business and collect business cards, was not really networking at all according to our new definition. It was more an attempt at marketing, selling or schmoozing. It may have resulted in leads, but not in trusted relationships.

Obtaining sales leads may sound like a worthwhile goal, but more often than not, these leads "lead" to nowhere. Time can be far better spent developing relationships by giving to others.

That's the difference between leads and referrals. Leads come from quick and impersonal marketing tactics that too often "lead" to a waste of time. Referrals come from people with whom you have built a relationship. When your contacts "refer" you to someone, they put their own reputation on the line. They are vouching for you based on the relationship you have developed over time.

Social Capital

Another concept associated with the Relationship Age and our new definition of networking is Social Capital. Not tangible like financial capital, it is still a commodity of great value. Social Capital refers to wealth in the form of intangible resources that an individual holds, resources like information, ideas, business opportunities, network of contacts, power, emotional support, trust and goodwill. Social Capital is built with others over time and with trust in one another.

Social Capital is especially important because it is an intangible resource that can be converted easily into something with real monetary value – a business deal, a job or a loan.

One of my favorite examples of the power of Social Capital comes from the European banking world. At the height of his wealth and success, Baron de Rothschild, the financier, was asked by an acquaintance for a loan. Reputedly, the great man replied, "I will not give you a loan myself, but I will walk arm in arm with you across the floor of the stock exchange and you will soon have willing lenders to spare."

Just being seen with this great man, whose personal reputation and character were as great as his financial wealth, implied to others that the companion with whom he chose to associate was as good as gold.

Applying the concept of Social Capital to networking, we see how Social Networks have value. Just as Baron de Rothschild converted his Social Capital into loans for an acquaintance, we also can convert our network of contacts into loans, new business, employment opportunities, political support, consensus building to drive decisions amongst a group and many more expressions of tangible value. Other people see us as "go to" people, the ones who can be relied on to get the job done. We have a certain power, which began with our choice and commitment to focus on giving rather than receiving.

The development of Social Capital goes hand in hand with effective networking. I encourage you to try it. As you grow your network of contacts and interact with them in a way highlighting giving rather than receiving, you boost the way people see you. You will see your value rising and your reputation expanding. As you increase your connections, add value to your relationships and give to others, your Social Capital improves and so does your personal brand.

The Role of Social Media

Still another indicator of the advent of the Relationship Age and one that millions of individuals and organizations around the globe are using is Social Media. Any study of networking today requires a look at the role of Social Media, examining just where and how it fits into the picture.

In simplest terms, Social Media is content created by people using highly accessible publishing technologies. It is a powerful element in the communication mix because it represents a shift in how people discover, read and share news, information and content. It is a fusion of sociology and technology, transforming monologues (one to many) into dialogues (many to many) and it represents the democratization of information, transforming people from content readers into publishers. Social Media has become extremely popular because it allows people to connect in the online world to form relationships for personal and business use.

The term "Social Networking" refers specifically to the building of online communities of people who share interests or activities or who are interested in following the activities of others. Most Social Networks provide a variety of ways for users to interact, such as email, text messaging and instant messaging.

Social Networking websites are used regularly by millions of people worldwide and include such sites as Facebook, MySpace, Twitter and LinkedIn to name a few.

The big question is: How valuable are these sites in building relationships and enhancing the strength of your networks?

The jury is still out, but much is being written about the potential value of social networking sites. Large corporations use them to track mention of the company's name, to see what people are saying, to do their own low-cost public relations and provide customer service.

An article in Business Week stated, "A growing number of companies are keeping track of what's said about their brands."[1] It went on to quote a leading technology expert who said, "The real control of the brand has moved into the customer's hands and technology has enabled that." Airlines, for example, use the social networking sites to track what customers are saying about

---

[1] Rachel King, "How Companies Use Twitter to Bolster Their Brands," *Business Week,* September 6, 2008.

them, to provide information on flight delays or cancellations and to throw some positive public relations into the mix.

In an article on the popular microblogging site, Twitter, Time Magazine commented on the "unsuspected depth" of hearing about what your friends had for breakfast. Technology writer Clive Thompson calls this "ambient awareness."[2] By following quick, abbreviated status reports from members of your social network, you get a "strangely satisfying glimpse of their daily routines."

All this said, one must ask what role Social Media might play in the average person's efforts to build networks of contacts and positive relationships. Here are a few possible uses:

- **Learning about your contacts** – Reading what they do, what they write about and what interests them.

- **Positioning Yourself and establishing your brand** – Describing who you are and what you do in a way that is consistent with how you want people in your network to perceive you.

- **Learning about competition** – Following those who provide similar products and services to you to learn what they are doing, how they position themselves.

- **Raising awareness of your expertise** – Publicizing your business or organization; providing links to videos of presentations you have given and articles you have written.

- **Creating a buzz** – Generating excitement around special activities, news items and the word on the street.

---

[2] Steven Johnson, "How Twitter Will Change the Way We Live," *Time*, Friday, June 5, 2009.

Having said all this, the question still exists: Is Social Networking worth the investment of time? Is your time better spent sending mass messages via computer and text messaging or by building relationships through personal interactions with individual contacts?

Only you can find the right balance between Social Networking and traditional networking, but remember, despite the appeal of online networking, the essence of "Effective Networking In The Relationship Age" is still the personal connection – the face-to-face meeting, handshake, phone call, pat on the back and handwritten note. This very gesture says, "I care about you, personally."

All of which brings us back to the challenge before us.

The Most Cost-Effective Solution

What is the most cost-effective solution to the challenge of finding and connecting with people who may need or value what you have to offer? My experience and the experiences of the people I have worked with is that it is not spending thousands of dollars on impersonal marketing and advertising that generates leads with a low probability of panning out. Nor, is it spending thousands of hours communicating with masses of people via technology.

My experience is that the most cost-effective way to achieve one's goals is through the personal development of strategic alliances and mutually beneficial relationships that result in the betterment of BOTH parties. This is the networking solution and this is what we will learn to master now.

THE SEVEN STEPS TO EFFECTIVE NETWORKING

*"Success is a process
more than a realization."*

~ Anonymous

With a clear vision of what networking is and why it is important, the focus shifts to the "how." How can we become effective networkers in the Relationship Age?

To answer this question, I have spent many hours studying hundreds of professional people with whom I interacted during my career and I noticed something interesting.

The people who achieved the best results were those who took specific actions as part of an integrated process and applied them with regularity. Individuals who took some of the steps, but not others, or applied them sporadically rather than consistently, showed fewer positive results.

Understanding the value of relationships, recognizing the interconnection between words and actions and knowing how to build credibility with others are all trademarks of a successful networker, but they are not enough. The most successful networkers follow a process.

The word "process" has come to have a special meaning for me. It is defined as "a series of actions, functions or steps which bring about a result."

Over the years, as I have continued my research and increased my own knowledge and expertise around networking, I truly understand how important a process is to successful networking. I realized that a system for effective networking could be put into practice by teaching people to embrace and consciously implement functions that most people already know and perform unconsciously. I have identified the Seven Steps in this process and how they are organized.

The steps are universally applicable, regardless of profession, cultural setting or products and services. Whether you are an individual business entrepreneur or part of a large organization or team, you will find that these steps deliver results. Whether Japanese, Canadian or Brazilian, you will find that this process applies in the varied circles within which you circulate. Only the contacts and their specific interests change. The steps remain the same.

Step One: Identify Your Networks

The first step in my Effective Networking Process is to *Identify Your Networks*. It involves taking inventory of your existing networks and the people within them. Most people are members of multiple networks and may not realize it. This step helps you identify those networks and select the people whom you want to include in your own personal networks.

This step is important because it prepares you to start from "day one" with networks that are effective and that you will want to grow and work with over time. It provides guidelines for identifying the right people to include and the information about them that will facilitate the networking process.

Step Two: Document Your Contacts

The second step – *Document Your Contacts* – is the foundation of the networking process. A well-documented database is one of your most valuable assets.

Having accurate information on your contacts is the key to the success of your networking. Having an easy-to-use method to document, store, organize and manage your contact information is fundamental. Step two outlines how to establish this essential structure upon which your networking efforts will depend.

Step Three: Evaluate Your Networks

Once you have created an initial database of contacts in your networks, you will want to implement the third step, which is to *Evaluate Your Networks.* This step is about understanding and assessing your networks and contacts so you will be in a better position to tap those resources in ways which bring the most value to everyone.

Understanding your networks and the way people relate to one another will make you a more effective networker.

Step Four: Position Yourself

No matter how many different networks you have, they all have one common ingredient – **YOU**! That is why Step Four is to *Position Yourself.* It focuses on establishing yourself as an expert in your field so everyone within your spheres of influence turns to you for information in your area of expertise.

Positioning Yourself as an expert in your field will have tremendous benefits. You will gain credibility with your clients. You will increase your visibility with broader target audiences, expand your outreach and attract new contacts. You will gain an edge over your competition and stand out amongst the crowd. Most important, you will clearly see how you can bring true added value to the relationships you develop with your contacts.

Step Five: Work Your Networks

Once you have established your own position, you are ready for Step Five, which is to *Work Your Networks*. This is nothing more than taking simple daily actions to increase the value and effectiveness of your networks and the people in them. It is the work you will do – day in and day out – to connect with the people in your networks and nurture the relationships.

As the world moves into the Relationship Age, the people who will be most successful are those who make a regular practice of reaching out and connecting with others.

Step Six: Improve Your Networks

The sixth step – *Improve Your Networks* – is about improving the quality and quantity of contacts in your networks. The step encompasses techniques for adding new contacts to your database while continuously evaluating and upgrading existing contacts.

Bigger and better networks produce bigger and better results. Step Six provides ideas for continuous improvement.

Step Seven: Maximize Your Networks

Step Seven provides the winning edge by showing how to *Maximize Your Networks*. It reveals what you can do to go the extra mile and make the most of your networks.

Repeatedly, the difference between those who achieve their goals consistently and those who just miss the mark is a matter of inches, seconds or even just a tiny bit of extra effort. Step Seven offers specific ideas on how to maximize your networks to greatest success.

Applying the Process

No one wants to spend money or time unnecessarily to attract new business, to meet new clients, to accomplish whatever goals are important in business and life.

Now, through my Effective Networking Process, we can develop strong networks of contacts to help achieve our dreams in a way that is powerful, cost-effective and enjoyable.

Of course, it does not just happen overnight or automatically. It takes commitment and hard work. It is a continuing process. Use of the concepts – and the results they bring – will eventually fade away if they are not continuously used and reinforced. The good news is we have the recipe that works. Our only job is to learn and apply it and, then, to enjoy the benefits that follow.

STEP ONE:
IDENTIFY YOUR NETWORKS

"Each friend represents a world in us,
a world possibly not born until they arrive."

~ Anais Nin

The first step in my Effective Networking Process is to identify your networks and the people in them.

The good news is that you already have and use networks; you just may not realize it. Or, you may realize it and wonder why you have to go through a formal process of clearly identifying them. Isn't just knowing they exist enough?

The answer is no. It is essential to inventory your networks and the people in them so:

1. You can evaluate your networks in a way that maximizes their effectiveness

2. You can more easily find the right person for the right job

3. You can more easily identify people you want to introduce to each other

Now, you may be thinking that you have only one network. That's a common belief. The truth is, most people have many networks. Some of those networks will intersect and some contacts will be members of two or more networks. That is why it is so important to develop a clear picture of your networks and who belongs to which.

The process for doing this is very easy and involves four simple actions or techniques:

1. Identify networks to which you belong.

2. Identify other members of those networks.

3. Classify those members and identify the ones you wish to add to your networks.

4. Obtain basic information on contacts in your networks.

Let's look at each technique.

1. Identify networks to which you belong.

Make a list of all the networks to which you belong. If you need help, you may want to consider the following general categories:

- Family
- Children Related
- Friends/Social
- Business/Professional
- Civic/Community
- Education
- Sports/Hobby Related
- Clubs
- Professional Associations
- Client Groups

A quick look at these headings probably makes you realize that you are indeed a member of many different networks.

When listing the networks to which you belong, do not hold back. Also, be specific. If you are a member of three or four different clubs, list each one by name. Each is separate and represents a separate network of contacts.

For a visual perspective of the networks to which you belong, take a large sheet of paper and draw a circle for each network. If some networks overlap, show that by having the circles overlap as in Figure 1-1. It is very common to have a circle of friends who are part of more than one group.

Figure 1-1.

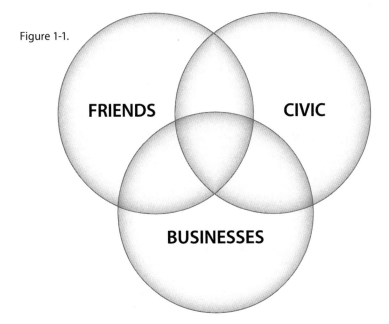

The networks you list represent a portfolio of relationships. Some of the members of these groups you may have known all your life and others may be very recent acquaintances. The important thing is these groups will form the foundation of a systematic way to add value to the lives of others and reap business success at the same time.

2. Identify other members of those networks.

Now that you have the group names listed, the next action or technique is to identify the individuals who are part of those networks. You do not have to add them to your network yet, but gather or make lists that represent the members of each group.

Once you have obtained lists of all the members of the networks that you are a part of, you are ready to do a validity check.

Your networks should include all the people you are acquainted with as well as the owners of businesses you interact with on a daily basis. A good validity check for the completeness of your lists is to go through old address books, Roladex files and holiday card lists to see if you find any names of contacts who are still current. Be sure to check any network groups which you might have missed. If so, add them now. Once you have a complete collection of lists of members of networks to which you belong, you are ready for the next action.

3. Classify those members and identify the ones you wish to add to your networks.

Technique three is to review all the lists you gathered above to identify the specific members from each network group that you belong to and that you want to add to your personal networks database.

You will not want to add everyone. For example, you may be part of a club that has 100 members. You may not want to add all of the members to your own personal contact list for that club, but only the 10 to 20 members with whom you have the closest connections.

So, how do you choose whom to add and whom not to add? One method I use to decide what contacts to add to my personal networks is the "A-B-C-D Method" and it literally is as simple as knowing your A, B, C's. You simply go through your lists of network contacts. For each contact, you assign them a letter rating. The ratings have absolutely nothing to do with them as individual human beings and are not personal in any way. Rather, they are rankings that reflect the relationship between each contact and you. Figure 1-2 includes a description of the four rankings.

The A-B-C-D Method of ranking contacts is extremely valuable for several reasons:

1. It provides a systematic approach and level of objectivity to your selection process, which may be applied to all networks regardless of how different they are.

2. It results in a guide that identifies the nature of the relationship you have with each contact in your networks and, by doing so, provides a framework for how you interact with that person and how you can add value to the relationship.

3. It enables you, with a quick glance, to know which contacts require further development and which ones are your true champions.

As you rate each contact, keep in mind that this is not a competition and it does not matter how many contacts you have in each category, just as it does not matter how many contacts you have in total.

For most people, the "A" group is the smallest and the "B" group is second smallest. As you begin to develop your networks, the "C" group may become the largest. At this point, however; since you are beginning with people who are part of your existing networks, the "C" and "D" groups may be small or nonexistent.

Just so you know, the average person has about 200 to 250 contacts in their database. Of course, this varies by individual and you will likely have fewer contacts at this point, since you are just getting started in identifying your networks.

Whatever the size of your networks, classifying and selecting your contacts gives you the foundation for your networking success.

Figure 1-2:

The A-B-C-D Method
for Classifying Contacts

A Contact – This is a top customer or client. It is someone who is loyal to you and will go out of his or her way to refer others to you. It is someone with whom you have a "strong tie" – a person with whom you are in close touch and who is one of your true champions.

B Contact – This is a loyal customer, client or supporter who has or would be happy to provide you with a referral. It is someone you consider a close contact even though you may only speak occasionally.

C Contact – This is a person you have met somewhere or know via someone else. If a business contact, you have not yet done business with them nor received a referral from them. For a non-business contact, it is someone who, in networking terms, is considered a "weak tie." It is a person who is not part of any networks in which you currently participate.

D Contact – You got the name and information about this person from somewhere or someone, but you can't remember or have never been in touch with them. You need to determine whether you can develop a relationship with this contact or if they should be removed from your database.

4. Obtain basic information on contacts in your networks.

Now you have a list of your own network contacts. This brings us to the final technique – obtaining basic information about the contacts in your network.

This action is essential because these individuals are the foundation of your networking efforts. You need to know as much as you can about them, but let's start with the basics.

By the way, if you are already up and running on a database system, you can start entering this information directly into your database. Otherwise, I recommend using common 3" x 5" index cards to record the information. These index cards can then be used to enter the information into your database. (More on this in the next chapter.) For now, your focus is on obtaining the information for each contact and having it in some form at your fingertips.

The basic contact data you need is identified in Figure 1-3. If you have additional information such as family member names or other relevant information, include that also. We will talk more about this in the next chapter. For now, however, your real concentration should be on getting the basics.

Figure 1-3
Basic Contact Data

Basic contact data should include:

- Name, including titles and nicknames
- Company name and address
- Home address
- All phone numbers – business, home, mobile and fax
- Email addresses (business & Personal and web addresses
- Birthday and place
- Hometown

By the way, you may wonder why you need a birth date, place and hometown and be tempted to skip this. **Do not!** These pieces of information are very important. Remember that these people represent the foundation of your networking database. If you truly want to be an effective networker, you should have all of these key pieces of information for every single one of your contacts.

Once you have finished obtaining basic information on the contacts in the networks you have identified, you are ready to go on to Step Two – Documenting Your Contacts.

First, you may want to take a break. You deserve it. You have just taken the first step to becoming an effective networker. Congratulations!

STEP TWO:
DOCUMENT YOUR CONTACTS

"You must look into people, as well as at them."
~ Lord Chesterfield

Having accurate information on your contacts is essential to the success of your networking. It is not how many people you know but what you know about them that matters. The more you know about someone, the easier it will be to add value to their lives and form a true quality relationship.

As you collect information about your contacts and continue to add new contacts to your networks, having an easy-to-use method to document, store, organize and manage your contact information is fundamental. That is why Step Two in my Effective Networking Process is to document your contacts.

For many professionals, the well-documented database is the entire business. Think about it. When doctors or dentists sell a practice, they are really selling their client list. Typically, the other aspects of their business are leased or have no significant value. On the other hand, a well-developed and well-documented database of current clients, past clients and potential clients will add significant value to a business or to an individual employee's value within a larger company. This is why Step Two is so important.

The process for developing an effective database is straightforward and encompasses four techniques:

1. Choose a database program.
2. Enter basic information about your contacts.
3. Identify the network designation(s) for each contact.
4. Identify additional information to be obtained.

Let's examine each.

1. Choose a database program.

Most everyone today uses an electronic database management system to store and manage contact information. If you do not currently use such a system, now is the time to start. There are wonderful programs from which to choose, ranging from such popular programs as Microsoft Outlook to more sophisticated Contact Management Systems.

If you are in the market for a new program, I recommend you do some online research and speak with representatives in local technology stores or other technology experts you know. Identify the features that are important to you. Some people, for example, want the ability to modify a database by adding new elements to a screen. Others want a program that can be used by multiple users or integrated with other programs and technologies, including mobile phones. Others are looking for simplicity of structure and the ease of use.

When choosing a program, the best advice I can give is to select a program that you feel comfortable using, that has most of the major features and is universally compatible with other software platforms.

My second recommendation, once you have chosen your program, is to become an expert in using it. So many people have a program but never really take the time to learn how to use it to its maximum capacity. Take a class. Buy a book. Whatever works best for you, learn how to work with your database program. Investing the time up front will save you hours of frustration later.

2. Enter basic information about your contacts.

Okay, so you have your program and you know how to use it. Now you are ready for the second technique – entering basic information about your contacts.

There is nothing really complicated about this. It will take some time. Establish your own rhythm and sequence for entering the data. Be consistent. Accuracy is important. You don't want to discover later an incorrect phone number or email address.

3. Identify the network designation(s) for each contact.

The third technique is one you may want to do while you are creating the new contact records and entering the basic contact information as part of technique two. Or, you may prefer to do it as a separate action after you have created the contact records. Either way, the important thing is to make sure you do it. Make sure that every contact in your database is designated as belonging to at least one network, or "category" as they are called in some database programs. Be sure to add the A-B-C-D Method as described in Step One.

Many of your contacts will belong to two or more networks. Your contact records should indicate this. This will be important information later when you start working with your contacts. Again, be diligent. A well-maintained database will pay off later!

4. Identify and obtain additional information.

Finally, you have all your existing contacts and basic information about them entered into your database system.

Now it is time to begin expanding on the information you have about each contact. Remember, the more you know about people, the more opportunity you will have to add value to their lives.

Following is a list, organized by general topic, of important information you should try to obtain and add to each contact record.

Education

1. High school and year graduated.
2. College. Graduated when, degrees in.
3. College honors. Any advanced degrees.
4. Fraternity or sorority.
5. Sports played or enjoyed.
6. Extracurricular activities.
7. If they didn't go to college. Any other types of education and are they sensitive about it.
8. Military service. Discharged when. Rank.
9. Attitude about being in the service now and then.

Family

1. Marital status. Spouses, significant other name.
2. Spouses, significant other Job, education.
3. Spouses, significant other interests. Hobbies. Affiliations.
4. Wedding anniversary.
5. Children. Names and Birthdates.
6. Children's education.
7. Children's hobbies and sports.

Business History

1. Previous employment and roles.
2. Any preferred status symbols.
3. Member of any trade or professional associations.
4. Mentors or people they admire.
5. How do they feel about their company. Industry.
6. Long range goals and business objectives.
7. Immediate needs or concerns.

Special Interests

1. Clubs or Service clubs such as Kiwanis or Masons etc.
2. Politically active.
3. Active in their community.
4. Religion and activity in such.
5. Sensitive about religion.
6. On what subjects or issues does contact have strong feelings negative or positive.

Lifestyle

1. Medical conditions.
2. Does contact drink
3. If so what. How much. When.
4. Smoke. Offended by smoking.
5. Favorite places for dining out.
6. Favorite foods and drink.
7. Hobbies and recreational interests.
8. Is contact a reader. Newspapers. Magazines. Books.
9. Favorite vacation places.
10. Kinds of cars owned.
11. Conversational interests.
12. Any hot buttons.
13. What words would you use to describe their personality.
14. Most proud of.
15. Goals.

You may be thinking, "Why on earth would I want to know all this information?" Or, "How am I going to get all this information?" The answer to these questions is the same and it is relatively easy. You want this information and you will obtain it because you care about this person. You want to cultivate a meaningful relationship with them. You want to get to know them. You want to add value to their life. You will obtain this information by having conversations with them over time.

Yes, obtaining this information about your contacts will be challenging. It won't happen all at once. It will take time. Above all, it will be an enjoyable experience and it will open doors to opportunities you could never imagine.

STEP THREE:
EVALUATE YOUR CONTACTS

*"People have one thing in common;
they are all different."*

~ Robert Zend

A comprehensive database of contacts in your networks is the starting point to your success as an effective networker. However, having accurate information on the people in your networks is powerful only if you know how to use the information. That is what Step Three is about – understanding and evaluating your networks and the contacts within them.

By evaluating your networks, you will be in a better position to find the right person for the right job or challenge and you will have greater success in bringing groups together. Understanding your networks and the way people in them relate to one another will make you a more effective networker.

The process for evaluating your networks is composed of four techniques:

1. Identify network types.
2. Map your networks.
3. Identify special players.
4. Assess your networks on seven key attributes.

Let's begin with a look at your network types.

1. Identify network types.

Networks can be broken down and identified in many different ways. While you have already given a specific title or category heading to each of your networks, you can also evaluate those networks according to different factors such as the role that the members of each network play in your business and your life.

For example, some networks are probably career-oriented and others may be social. Some may be strong support networks for you and others may be important sources of information and expertise. Here are some of the most popular networks:

Career Networks – These networks are composed primarily of people in your career field. They are the people you rely on for advice about your career and work life. They include business colleagues, mentors, close advisors at work and members of professional associations in your career field.

Task Networks – These networks include people who help you accomplish things and get your job done. They are not in your specific career field, but they have talents and skills that complement your own expertise. They may include your accountant, attorney, technology adviser and people in other departments or organizations.

Social Networks – These are your friends and family – the people who are not part of your work life, but who provide companionship and interpersonal interaction in your life.

Knowledge Networks – These people have specific knowledge and expertise in special fields. They are Subject Matter Experts and you rely on them for their knowledge.

Referral Networks – These people are individuals who make a lot of referrals, people who introduce you to others. They are not bound together in any specific network category, but come from many of your primary networks. You can consider them your "referral network" because, whether these individuals come from your business life or personal life, they provide the most referrals.

Entrepreneurial Networks – This network consists of people you consider entrepreneurs – individuals who organize, operate and assume the risks of operating a business. They often offer fresh thinking, sound advice and suggestions on important resources.

Influencer Networks – The people in this network are not primary decision makers, but they have the ability to influence decisions. They may come from your business or personal life and networks and they are participants in this network because they have one important quality in common – the ability to influence others.

Support Networks – These are the people who compose your primary support system. They are probably the people you are closest to and interact with frequently. They include family members, friends and possibly close business associates – the people who are there for you - day in and day out - and whenever you need them.

Understanding these different types of networks and the roles the people within them play is an important part of evaluating the effectiveness of your networks. It will help you see the strengths in your networks and where you may have gaps. Perhaps you need to recruit more people in your knowledge network or referral network. Perhaps your networks are all work and no play. Assessing your networks from this perspective will help you gain an understanding about the strengths and weaknesses of your networks, so you can act appropriately to improve them.

2. Map your networks.

The next technique is to map your networks to gain an understanding of how the members of your networks fit together and what roles they play. The deeper the understanding you have of each person, the easier it will be to find ways to help one another and to share information.

Mapping your entire network can be overwhelming, so I suggest you begin with your top 10 to 20 contacts and add to your map over time as you see the value of the mapping process. Start with the people you rely on the most for their expertise and advice – the ones you share information with on a regular basis.

One way to visualize a "Network Map" is to construct it as a group of circles, with overlapping circles for individuals who are members of multiple networks. I also recommend a second option.

Take a large sheet of paper and divide it into three vertical columns. Label the columns, from left to right: Contact Name, Introduced By and Introduced To.

1. In the left column, list the names of the contacts. Include a few brief notes about the kinds of information you share, how frequently you communicate with each other and how strong a tie you have with them.

2. In the middle column, write down who introduced you to the contact or where and how you met them. If someone else did not introduce you, write "self" in that column.

3. In the right column, list whom you have introduced that contact to. If you have not connected them with someone else, leave a blank spot.

Once you have your list with the three columns completed, sit back and look at it from a broader perspective. Look for trends by answering questions that follow:

- Did you meet most of your contacts yourself or did someone else introduce you?

- Are there particular people whose names appear frequently in the middle column – people who have introduced you to a number of your contacts?

- Are the people you meet through these individuals' strong contacts or weak contacts? Do you communicate frequently or infrequently?

- Are there particular places or events where you tend to meet more contacts?

- Are the people you meet at some events stronger contacts than the people you meet at other events?

- Do the people who you meet through certain people or at certain places share more information than those you meet through others or by yourself?

- Looking at the right column, do you tend to introduce your contacts to other people or do you have blanks in this column?

- Do you tend to introduce certain kinds of contacts more often than others do? If yes, what kind?

- Do you tend to introduce contacts at certain events or locations more than others do? If yes, where?

- What other observations or trends can you identify from the information on this Network Map?

As you observe, I strongly recommend you note them, then, add observations about specific people in your networks that play special roles.

Finally, after reviewing your observations, make a list of appropriate action plans. For example, if you observed that you are introduced to a lot of new people, but that you rarely introduce your contacts to others, you may develop an action plan to "introduce at least x number of contacts to other people in your networks each month." Remember, it is better to give than to receive. If you help your contacts expand and strengthen their networks, they will be more likely to reciprocate. On the other hand, if you notice the contacts you meet through a certain individual are stronger than contacts you meet through others, you may want to do something special for that person.

As you can see, it is in this analysis and action plan phase the true value of mapping is realized. The overview you receive from your Network Map can be invaluable. It can help you eliminate time-consuming activities that do not pay off. It can help you focus your networking activities on people and activities which show the greatest results. It can prevent you from networking blindly by shining a light on the networking interactions, which prove most beneficial.

3. Identify special players.

Having a clear map of your networks will allow you to identify the type of contacts you have and the roles different people play.

Let's look first at the type of contacts. In Step Two, you may recall using the A-B-C-D Method to classify members of various networks to determine which members you wanted to add to your personal networks. Now that you have chosen the members of your own networks, the philosophy behind the A-B-C-D Method still applies.

In simplest terms, you have two types of contacts in your networks – Strong Contacts and Weak or Casual Contacts:

Strong Contact – This type of contact is someone with whom you are very close. Family members, personal friends, partners, close business associates and perhaps top clients fall into this category. These Strong Contacts provide a tight circle in which you work a good part of the time. These contacts supply you with most of the information you use. They are your "go to" people and constitute your high quality, loyal contacts.

Casual Contact – This type of contact includes everyone else, the people with whom you have weaker ties and a more casual relationship. Past customers, personal and professional acquaintances, vendors and others you do not know as well fall into this category. Frequently, you may not be as close to these people because, while they are a part of your network, they are also highly involved in and members of other networks.

Remember, regardless of what role people in your network may play, everyone is either a Strong Contact or a Casual Contact.

The Role of Information Brokers

As you examine the information on your Network Map, you will undoubtedly see the names of certain people reappearing several times. These people are most likely individuals who play the role of "Information Brokers" – people who have the power to shape the opinions and decisions of others.

By focusing on Information Brokers and spending more time with them, you can greatly increase your ability to spread the word about yourself and your services.

What are Information Brokers? They are people who spread information, helping information jump from one network to another. They are known as "Connectors" because they connect one network to another. Without these Connectors, information is trapped within each network or cluster of individuals.

One of the most important tasks you can perform is to review your Network Map and identify specific individuals in your networks who are Information Brokers. Then, you will want to take this a step further by identifying what kind of Information Broker they are. Knowing what roles people play will give you a better understanding of how to make the most of your interactions with them. The better you know your contacts, the better your ability to add value to your relationships.

Information Brokers or Connectors can be identified in a variety of ways – by the type of Connector they represent, by certain labels they use, by common characteristics and by professions. These methods provide hints to help us identify these important people in our lives.

Let's start with the concept of "Hubs." Connectors are often referred to as Hubs because they serve as a center of activity or interest. They are people who communicate with others on a regular basis and the type of hub they represent can sometimes identify them:

- **Regular Hub** – Individuals who serve as a regular hub are ones who are connected to people in one to several different networks.
- **Mega Hub** – Individuals who interact with a wide range of people in multiple networks. They are considered opinion and thought leaders and include media professionals, politicians and celebrities.
- **Expert Hub** – These individuals have specific and significant knowledge in a particular field and are highly connected to others in that realm and spread that knowledge to a multitude of other networks.
- **Social Hub** – These are the social butterflies who seem to know everyone in various social worlds. They are highly charismatic, very socially active and move easily between different networks.

You may also identify Information Brokers who are referred to by certain labels such as:

- **Thought and Opinion Leaders** – Individuals who shape the thinking and opinions of others.
- **Subject Matter Experts and Mavens** – Subject Matter Experts and Mavens are people who have a great deal of knowledge, skill and talent in a particular area.
- **Influencers and Buzz Creators** – Just as the name implies, these people are highly social and bring a sense of excitement to products, services and concepts.
- **Early Adopters** – An early adopter or lighthouse customer is an early customer of a given company, product, or technology. In politics, fashion and art, this person might be referred to as a trendsetter. These people are often Information Brokers because, in addition to using a new product or service, they will also provide considerable and candid feedback on a product or service.

Whatever their label, people who play the role of Information Brokers, Connectors or Hubs can often be identified by these common characteristics:

- They are connected to many people in many different walks of life and many different networks.
- They expose themselves to new information from a variety of sources.
- They are people others rely on for information or expertise.
- They travel extensively and meet new people.
- They are outgoing and engage people in conversation.

Still, another way to identify Information Brokers is by their profession. Here are some common professions of Connectors:

- **Restaurant Owners** – They are always meeting and feeding new people and are highly connected. They feed celebrities, politicians, athletes, community leaders and people from multiple networks.

- **Recruiters** – Employment recruiters, or head hunters, know a lot of people in many varied professions. Help them and they will help you. They are talent scouts, always looking for new talent.

- **Politicians & Lobbyists** – These folks have massive databases and attend many events which put them in front of people. They are connected to power and wealth.

- **Fundraisers** – These people are professional networkers whose job it is to meet a lot of people in their efforts to raise money for various causes.

- **Journalists** – These professionals interact with all kinds of people and are skilled in obtaining and reporting information.

- **Celebrities** – Whether actors, athletes, musicians, authors, artists or some other profession, people who are celebrated for their achievements are exposed to many others and frequently share information with the public.

Now, you have some tips for how to identify Information Brokers and the roles they play. Finally, I would like to share one last and very powerful concept with you.

The Strength of Weak Ties

Thinking back to our earlier distinction between Strong Contacts and Casual Contacts, you might expect your strongest contacts or ties to be your Information Brokers and Super Connectors. This is not necessarily true.

In his theory on the "Strength of Weak Ties," American sociologist, Mark Gravonetter, explains, people who are your weakest contacts or ties may actually be the best Connectors. Why? Because they are often members of multiple networks. People we do not deal with on a consistent basis and who are part of multiple networks can have a lot of power because they provide us with fresh information that comes from outside our normal networks. On the other hand, our Strong Contacts may be our closest contacts because they are the core of our primary network and they do not spend as much time interacting with other people in other networks. Think about it. How uncanny – our Casual Contacts may offer the greatest goldmine of networking opportunities!

4. Assess your networks on seven key attributes.

The fourth technique for evaluating your networks is to assess them on seven key elements that are required for successful connections.

The first three of these characteristics focus on you. After all, it is likely you, yourself, may be a Hub or Connector of one or more of your networks and you have the power to jump and spread information from one network to another. It is important that you possess these first three attributes.[3]

---

[3] Adapted from *"The Virtual Handshake, Opening Doors and Closing Deals Online, "* by Scott Allen and David Teten.

The remaining four attributes relate to the quality of the c in your network database:

- **Character.** Your character is always the first and foremost when dealing with others. Are you known to be open, honest and caring? Are you viewed by others to be a person of integrity? This is essential. If your character is called into question even in the slightest degree, you will not be able to build trusting relationships.

- **Competence.** This refers to your professional skills and abilities. Your network needs to view you as the Subject Matter Expert for your given field of expertise. You can build this competence in the minds of others by communicating frequent and timely information. For example, your network should hear about changes or news in your field from you, rather than from newspapers, television, internet or any other source. Providing this information is a way to show your competence and provide added value to your contacts.

- **Relevance.** You need to be relevant to your contacts. This means providing information, introductions, referrals and other support which is timely and of current interest. It demonstrates your ability to contribute to the good of the group by the open sharing of information.

- **Information.** The information I am talking about here is the data you have on each of your contacts. This runs the range from the basics to what I call "High Value Information" such as the personal likes, dislikes and preferences of your contacts. Remember, it's not how many people you know; it's what you know about them that will allow you to add value to their lives.

- **Strength.** This is the strength of your ties. There are two major types. Strong and weak ties. You need both. The strong ties are those that you are in constant communication with on a regular basis. This is where 90 percent of the information flows within your core networks. The weak ties give you access to information from outside your primary networks, information to which you do not have normal access. The weak ties are the Casual Contacts you speak with infrequently but, when you do, you receive fresh information.

- **Number.** This is the total number of contacts in your database. Effective networking is more than a numbers game. The more people in your networks database, the more opportunity you have to develop meaningful relationships ultimately enriching your business and life.

- **Diversity.** Last, but not least, a good network has diversity. A strong network should have people that represent all major industries, goods and services. The diversity of your contacts should be shown in geography, industry, gender, political views and economic status. You want your network to have representatives as diverse as possible.

Examine your own networks; see if you have all seven of these attributes working for you. If not, you know now where to get started. Strengthening your networks is an ongoing process and, as this list of attributes shows, it begins with you – which leads us to one of the most exciting steps in the process of successful networking – **Positioning Yourself!**

STEP FOUR: POSITION YOURSELF

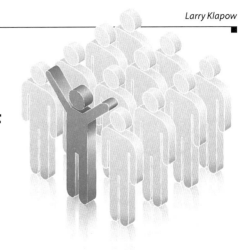

*"If people like you they'll listen
to you, but if they trust you
they'll do business with you."*
~ Zig Ziglar

Essential to the success within your networks is being viewed as an expert in your field. Specifically, you want to establish yourself so everyone within your spheres of influence thinks of you first and calls you for timely information in your area of expertise rather than going to the newspapers, television, internet or any other sources.

Positioning Yourself as an expert in your field will have such a powerful effect on your business success and will be so incredibly rewarding that it is well worth the effort. It will:

- **Create the trust** necessary for potential clients to feel comfortable and confident about purchasing your services, products and programs.

- **Gains you visibility** to reach all your target audiences.

- **Extends your outreach**, enabling you to get your message out to new audiences you would not normally have reached.

- **Establishes yourself as a first source** of timely and significant information so you are the first to come to mind when someone needs some kind of services, products or programs you offer.

- **Gives you an edge** over competitors and enables you to stand out from the crowd.

- **Helps you gain clients** and increases your fees as the demand for your services, products and programs increases.

Positioning Yourself as an expert in your field is an important ingredient to your success in networking. It involves two aspects: becoming an expert and establishing yourself as an expert.

Becoming an Expert

Before sharing techniques for how to Position Yourself as an expert, I think it is appropriate to say a few words about becoming an expert. Let's start with a definition. Just what is an expert anyway and what qualifies someone to be one? The dictionary defines an expert as "an individual with a high degree of skill in or knowledge of a certain subject or field; a specialist; authority; possessing skill or knowledge; trained by practice; skillful or skilled."

Many people are reluctant to label themselves as experts in fear that people will think they know everything. Let me assure you that you need not worry. No one knows everything. Nobody expects you to know everything. People expect you to be knowledgeable, to be interested and alert to new developments in your field and to have the integrity and commitment to say, "I don't know, but I will find out."

The important thing is to realize, in order to Position Yourself as an expert, you must first take steps to become reasonably well versed in your chosen field. Here are some suggestions:

techniques demonstrating your expertise in a particular topic or field. Specifically, I recommend these four techniques as part of Step Four – **Positioning Yourself:**

1. Teach others what you know.
2. Write articles.
3. Give presentations
4. Create buzz.

Let's examine each.

1. Teach others what you know.

One of the best ways to add value to the lives of others and increase your own credibility, as an authority on a particular subject, is to teach others what you know and what will be useful to them. When you play the role of an instructor, you are immediately viewed as an authority on the subject.

Now, you may be wondering how in the world you can get a teaching assignment. Let me tell you – it is not as difficult as you may think. Many organizations are looking for specialists to teach a variety of subjects, some paid assignments and some volunteer opportunities. Either way, the investment of your time is well worth it and can pay off handsomely in the future. Opportunities include:

- Local community colleges
- Local high school adult education programs
- City and community adult education programs
- YMCAs and community centers
- Private adult education programs such as the Learning Annex
- Corporations that sponsor in-house training for employees

The opportunities abound and making the effort to offer to teach a class, workshop or seminar is often welcomed with great enthusiasm. I once offered to teach workshops to employees of medium to large organizations in the employee break and lunch rooms. The sessions met with great success and were viewed by employees as a change of pace from the routine and a valuable investment by management in their ongoing learning and development.

Teaching is also a two-way street. Not only is it an opportunity for you to impart your knowledge, but it is a way for you to connect with people who are interested in your field and to learn from them. I am not necessarily talking about learning concepts and factual information, but learning about what people are most interested in, what they have questions about and what their needs related to your field are. Understanding your target market's needs and interests will help you do a better job of Positioning Yourself to address and answer those needs for others. Ask your students:

- What did you like best about this course?
- What was the one best thing you learned?
- What did you like least?
- What would you advise me to do differently?
- Was any part of the course particularly memorable?
- Are you comfortable recommending my services to others?

So many people who teach classes and give presentations miss the opportunity to garner support from the people in their audiences. Do not be one of them. Take advantage of this group of people while you still have their attention.

Finally, teaching produces unexpected and remarkable results. Early in my career, I was looking for a way to establish myself and increase my credibility as an expert in real estate. I signed up to offer a home selling clinic at my local community college. Shortly before the clinic was to begin, the college called me to advise me that only four people had signed up and, given the low enrollment; it would be okay to cancel the class. I thought about it and decided to tell the college I would go through with offering the clinic. I felt that my name was associated with the class, that the four people had paid their money and deserved to receive the information they wanted. I taught the four-hour clinic and walked away from it thinking it was great practice for public speaking and was an opportunity to hone my teaching skills.

One week later, I received a call from a woman who had attended my clinic. She had a beautiful property in my area she needed to sell quickly. I listed and sold the home within eight days for 1.2 million dollars, which was a LOT of money at the time. A week after, the property sale closed, I received a call from another student. She had inherited an estate property and needed it sold as soon as the market would allow. I listed and sold that property for $820,000. The seminar should have been cancelled, but was not. Due to my ethics and drive, I produced 2 million dollars in closed real estate deals and netted a sizable commission for myself.

The bottom line is this: Each one of your students is a potential new member of your network. These people will remember you as an expert on your subject and, when they need future help in that area, or are asked by someone else for a recommendation of someone who is an expert in that area, your name will be one of the first to come to mind. That is effective positioning and the results can be astounding.

2. Write articles.

A second technique for establishing yourself as an expert is writing. There is something very exciting about seeing your words in a mass publication.

You may be surprised how many editors are looking for fresh information and perspectives from freelance contributors; especially if they don't have to pay for it. Here are some of the most likely opportunities:

- **General Interest Publications** – Most general interest magazines clearly state what kinds of articles are of interest and how to contact them.

- **Business and Airline Publications** – Special categories unto themselves, these publications appeal directly to a captive business audience and have a large readership.

- **Trade Journals** – Perhaps the best opportunity lies with the huge array of professional journals and trade publications geared toward a particular field of interest. Having an article published is often easy and makes a huge impression on those outside your field to see you published and recognized by other experts in your field.

- **Newspapers** – Some weekly and monthly publications welcome special interest feature articles from writers. Also, do not neglect the OpEd section of major newspapers. A well-written opinion piece will reach thousands of readers and be posted on the newspaper's web site with your name and contact information.

- **Internet**–As the world moves to paperless communication, more and more people are reading their news and doing their research online. You will often reach them best through contributing to or creating your own monthly newsletter, news feed or blog.

Whatever outlets you choose for publishing your articles, do not be confined to traditional formats. Editors love fresh, creative thinking. For example, here is one of the tactics I used with great success. I wanted to be published in a local newspaper because I knew that was what people shopping for real estate read most. After reading the local papers for a few weeks, I noticed a popular weekly community publication never had any real estate information or articles, so I came up with a win/win plan for both of us. I proposed a one-third-page weekly article I would write, free of charge, on topical real estate information. The only thing I asked was that my name, email, phone number and photo be included at the end of the article. The benefit to them would be the articles would attract advertising from real estate and mortgage agencies they could place around the article. They agreed to try it and had amazing success! In a short time, the remainder of the page was filled with advertisements. By the second month, the advertisements spilled over to the adjacent second page. The editor was very happy. As for myself, within a few months, I was writing articles for three other community newspapers. Not the same article; which would have been easiest. I felt each publication deserved exclusivity. Before long, phone calls and emails were piling in. Anyone looking to buy real estate and who read one or more of these publications viewed me as the Subject Matter Expert.

Now, here is an important tip: Once your article appears in print, don't just sit back and wait for calls and emails to come in. Work it! Ask the publication to provide you with reprints of the article, or print your own. In my case, after writing for several months, I had a library of articles to use as handouts, post on my web site, include with correspondence and marketing materials, feature in company newsletters and even incorporate in future publications.

The benefits to writing articles are significant! You generate inquiries, create hard copy documentation of your expertise and now have an opportunity to research and reflect on topics of interest to you and your target audiences. Put the power of words to work for you!

3. Give presentations.

The thought of public speaking may stop you cold. You are not alone. One of the top fears among adults is the fear of public speaking. If you fall in this group, my best advice is to find a class or program to help your overcome this fear and hone your speaking skills. Toastmasters is a wonderful option. Just about every major city has a local club; it is inexpensive, a lot of fun and gives you a chance to expand your networks as you meet new people who are all working towards a common goal.

The ability to speak confidently to any size group is essential if you are to Position Yourself as an expert in your field. That is why it is so important for you to overcome your initial fears and begin making presentations. Start small, with a 30-second to one-minute practice speech and work your way up. Before you know it, you will not be able to stop! Believe me, there is nothing like the feel of having a whole room in the palm of your hand, hanging on your every word.

Seek out the opportunity to speak wherever you can, no matter how small the audience. Also, don't confine yourself to traditional, monologue-style speeches. Presentations come in all forms. Polish your PowerPoint and multimedia skills. Grant interviews and dialogues. Participate in debates and panel presentations. Here are just a few ideas for opportunities:

- **Professional Associations** – Volunteer to present on a project or success story with your peers.

- **Local schools** – Educators frequently welcome vocational experts into classrooms as guest presenters.

- **Clubs** – A vast array of clubs – social, political, service and special-interest – are always seeking speakers. The Commonwealth Club, Rotary Clubs, local civic and social clubs. The list is endless. Contact these organizations and offer your services.

- **Conferences and Conventions** – Most major national and international conferences have a "call for papers" in which you can submit an application to be selected as a speaker. Select conferences which are important in your field and submit not just one but multiple applications. If you are not chosen the first time, submit again the next time. The selection committee will begin to recognize your name and eventually select you.

- **TV and Radio Stations** – Many local news, special interest and talk show programs are looking for experts on specific topics of popular interest to interview. Do not wait for them to call you. Call them and volunteer to do an interview.

- **Speakers Bureaus** – As you become skilled and known as a speaker, you may want to register with one or more speaker's bureaus. The fees can be lucrative and these opportunities often put you in front of fresh audiences outside your normal spheres of influence.

Most of the information you will need about associations and organizations is on the internet. A variety of other resources exists as well. Do your homework. Find the audiences that are right for you - **Go Speak!**

Making presentations is one of the best ways to increase your visibility and credibility as an expert. Plus, it offers the opportunity to interact with your audience. Never miss the opportunity to take questions and learn what issues are on the minds of your audiences. In fact, when possible, look for ways to involve your audience from the beginning – via mini-surveys, questions with a show of hands, call-ins on radio programs, and identify ways to respond to specific needs and interests of your audience.

If you ever had a fear of public speaking, you will soon overcome it, because, as an effective networker, your focus will not be on yourself, but on the individual members of your audience so you can figure out how to use your considerable knowledge to help them best.

4. Create buzz.

As you establish yourself as an expert through teaching, writing and presenting, you have an opportunity to do some of the most powerful and least costly marketing possible. It is what I call "creating buzz" and it is based on word-of-mouth communication.

By gaining the trust and respect of the people you are communicating with, you are now in a position to get the word out about what you do and how you can help people. You will be surprised at how fast the good news travels. Remember, people want to do business with others they trust, know and like.

Creating buzz is nothing more than putting the wheels in motion to "create excitement and spread the word about your services, products, programs and ideas via referrals from others across traditional boundaries to reach people in multiple networks."

The benefits of creating buzz are amazing. Here are some of the things it does:

- Cuts through the media noise that exists today because almost everyone prefers to do business based on a referral from a delighted consumer versus a glitzy advertisement, sales pitch or other broad-spectrum marketing appeal that promises more than it may be able to deliver.
- Spreads like wildfire, bringing valid and timely business opportunities more quickly than you can imagine.
- Costs almost nothing.

- Increases the number of responses and inquiries almost exponentially. It is not just one person telling another. As excitement builds, it is one person telling many, each of whom tells many more and so on.

Quite simply, creating buzz is one of the most exciting ways available to position yourself as an expert in your field and to spread the word quickly to a large number of people about how you can help them. To be successful at creating a buzz, you need to focus on two things: crafting your message and transmitting your message.

Crafting Your Message

The first and perhaps best advice I can offer about crafting a message which will effectively create buzz is to make sure the information you convey responds to an important and timely need. Undoubtedly, you could select from among a significant variety of messages to convey about you, your services, products and programs. The key to creating buzz is to select ONE message, not several entangled together and one which specifically appeals to a need your target audience is experiencing now. The greater the need, the more likely your success in eliciting a response to a solution you can provide.

How do you know what people need? Look for clues. Read the paper, listen to television and radio, visit internet sites featuring news feeds and blogs to learn what people are talking about, what they have on their minds. That failing, ask them. Do a survey. If you are teaching a class or giving presentations, take time to ask people what needs are most pressing for them, what concerns they have, what issues are most on their minds.

If you have a web site, post a survey. Easy-to-use survey tools allow you to create and publish custom surveys in minutes and then view results. Whatever method you use, spend the time to clearly identify what topics will appeal to people's needs and inspire them to immediate action. Believe me; it will surprise you how quickly people become interested in something that speaks to their interests. I learned this lesson when I was teaching.

For me, it happened almost by chance. I had signed up to teach a class at the local community college. I was in an area where many young people were striving to purchase their first homes. I decided to call the class Homebuying 101. Wow! Did I ever choose a name that struck a chord? People were rushing to enroll in my class. Not only did I establish myself as an expert by teaching the class, but I created a buzz which spread like wildfire throughout the community. It made the college happy, saved numerous new prospective homebuyers from making expensive mistakes as they negotiated their way through their first home buying experience and resulted in some nice business for my firm.

If speaking to a direct need is the first criteria for an effective message, the second criterion is clarity. Make sure your message is phrased clearly and concisely and in a consistent and compelling manner. That is why sticking to one message is important. Look at advertisements for ideas on how to do this. The best advertisements convey one clear message. Those ads that try to combine two or more messages in one ad are less effective. Sometimes, you can add secondary messages as "add-ons," but the one primary message should be bold, front-and-center and impossible to mistake as the key point.

Finally, do not be afraid to highlight the unusual. News media, in particular and people in general love ideas that are offbeat and quirky. For example, I knew a real estate agent who had a very innovative idea. A few days after escrow closed, the agent would send a handyman over to the owners' new house, having paid for two hours of free service. Anyone who has moved into a new home knows the frustration of having just made the biggest purchase of your life and then having to deal with a squeaky door or dripping faucet. A small added value gesture like this turns you from a run-of-the-mill provider into a memorable service provider who cares. Furthermore, the unique nature of the service provides a great story containing a great message.

Transmitting Your Message

Now that you have your message clearly identified, your attention turns to how to transmit it. If your message is compelling enough, sometimes this will be out of your hands. Other people and media will take your message and run with it. To help it along, here are some ideas:

- **Develop and distribute a news release with a backup press package.** Anytime you have a newsworthy announcement, do not hesitate to develop a news release and send it to media, including your local newspapers and television stations. News media are always looking for fresh and interesting ideas that will appeal to their readers/viewers. The important factor here is timeliness. News media do not want a story on an event that happened last week. They want it a few days before the event so, if they are interested, they can cover it. If something exciting happened today, they want the write-up by the end of the day for tomorrow's news coverage. By the next day, it will be old news. When you send the news release, include a backup press packet and include your resumé or biography, a headshot of yourself, concise information on the services you provide and, if you have it, samples of prior articles you have published and announcements of classes you have taught or presentations you have given. It is a good idea to have multiple copies of this press packet on hand for times when you receive calls from media unexpectedly. Also, be sure to post your news releases and your press packet, on your web site.

- **Share the news with your Information Brokers.** Now is one of the times when the work you did to identify Information Brokers in your networks will pay off. Send a message or give a call to those Connectors, Hubs and casual contacts with connections to multiple networks to give them your news. Then, let them take it from there. Think about it… How did you first learn about your:

  - Doctor
  - Dentist
  - Hairdresser
  - Babysitter
  - Job
  - Spouse, partner or significant other

Chances are, you heard about them through a recommendation from a friend or someone you trust. Now is an opportunity for you to allow your contacts to spread your name and news to all of their friends. All you have to do is to put the word out on the street. Then, sit back and watch as the information travels through networks, neighborhoods and the business community.

- **Splash the news across your web site.** While the home page of your web site may remain fairly static most of the time, if you have timely and exciting news to share, this is a time to create a large and colorful announcement and post it on your home page with links to your news release, press packet and other relevant information. Just don't forget to remove it after the news is old. There is nothing worse than going to a web site that has a big announcement about an event that has already happened.

- **Send an email.** Use your list of contacts and make them feel special by sending them a special news alert with your message. The email can be brief and be sure to include a link to your news release and web site.

- **Take advantage of online media.** This is one time you may want to experiment with social networking. Place a brief and enticing comment on the many Social Media sites that are appropriate for your message and be sure to include a link to your web site. You may receive interest from well beyond your local area and normal spheres of influence.

- **Be creative.** Yes, as old as the phrase is, think outside the box. Try to think of creative ways to develop enthusiasm around your message. For example, everyone knows real estate open houses are held weekly, with homes open on different days and at different times. Frankly, the process was getting somewhat wearisome in the minds of my agents, not to mention prospective clients. I wanted to infuse some excitement, so I created an Open House Extravaganza – one time a year when every single listing the company had was held open on the same day.

The agents got extremely excited and went out of their way to provide refreshments and special touches at each open house. There was a real fervor in the air as clients went around from one house to the next. Although I created this event years ago, to this day, the company continues to hold the event and agents and clients alike look forward to it.

Positioning Yourself for the Fun

We have placed a great deal of attention on helping you establish yourself as an expert in your field, someone your contacts will feel comfortable with, turn to and trust. It is a critical element to establishing relationships of value with your contacts.

Whichever suggestions from Step Four you pursue – however you spread the word about the services, products and programs you offer – Positioning Yourself as a credible, trustworthy and accomplished expert in your field is essential to your networking success.

Once you establish yourself and clarify what it is you have to give to others, the real fun begins – the fun of sharing your gifts with the people who are part of your networks.

STEP FIVE:
WORK YOUR NETWORKS

*"Don't judge each day by the harvest you reap,
but by the seeds that you plant."*

~ Robert Louis Stevenson

Perhaps you have heard of a "runner's high." It is that euphoric state described by many runners when their bodies experience a release of endorphins, the brain's naturally occurring opiates, during a prolonged run. Runners and other athletes frequently describe the condition as feeling so ecstatic and at peace that it is as if they were under the influence of mind-altering drugs. They are calm, relaxed and filled with a deep sense of joy.

Now, a significant body of research conducted by social and scientific organizations confirms the existence of a phenomenon similar to the runner's high. It is what I call the "Giver's High." I define this condition as a feeling of "well-being and happiness experienced by people who help and give to others." The benefits, which have been documented by researchers, include:

- A measurable improvement in immune system functions

- Health benefits equivalent to those experienced by those who quit smoking, lose weight and lower their blood pressure

- Greater psychological well-being and stability in life

These studies also show that people who are less connected to others at home, in their communities and at work are more at risk of getting sick or experiencing stress and anxiety.

Now, more than ever, as people recognize the value of staying connected with one another, our society is moving closer and closer toward a true relationship economy. In the Relationship Age, those who are most successful will be those who are most adept at working their networks – those who are skilled at connecting with and reaching out to others. Fortunately, the process is beneficial and fun.

Working your networks is nothing more than taking simple actions to increase the value and effectiveness of your networks and the people in them. The process emphasizes four basic techniques:

1. Make referrals.
2. Send handwritten notes.
3. Implement the "**Daily Datum**." (More on this later.)
4. Nurture your inner circle.

Remember, each technique deserves special attention.

1. Make referrals.

Making referrals for others is the first and most important way for you to benefit your networks and yourself. I promise you this:

"If you spend more time looking for business for others than you do for yourself, soon, you will reap more rewards than you can handle."

The best news is the referrals you make and receive will all be of the highest quality. Remember earlier when we discussed the difference between a sales lead and a personal referral? A lead is a name with no personal connection behind it. A referral is recommending someone with whom you have built a relationship and for whom you are giving a personal guarantee based on that relationship. It is one of the highest quality recommendations possible.

You have probably heard to be truly successful, you should build a business 100% on referrals.. Most people will probably agree, but the challenge is that most people do not know how to build one.

Why not test your record? Try this little exercise: "What is your Referral Score?" Ask yourself these simple questions:

- What was the last referral you gave out?
- Do you remember the details and the people involved?
- What was the last referral you received?
- Do you remember the details of that transaction?
- Do you remember which of your contacts were involved?

If you do not remember the details of your last referrals, then chances are, you are not giving out enough.

After years of networking success, let me offer some tried and true tips on the art and science of referrals. These guidelines will provide a solid foundation for a lifetime of giving and receiving great referrals:

- **Look for opportunities.** Always keep your eyes and ears open. Listen for the needs of others. Train yourself to be on the lookout for opportunities to refer other businesses and professionals on a daily basis. Make it a fun game to see how many people you can help in a given day.

- **Ask what people need.** One of the most obvious and overlooked methods of generating referrals is to ask the individuals in your networks what services they use and need on a regular basis and what they may be in need of now.

- **Document your referrals.** Get in the habit of documenting all incoming and outgoing referral business. This will tie back to your Network Mapping and help you evaluate where and how to strengthen your networks.

- **Never refer for money.** When you refer another professional, you are vouching for that person and endorsing them. Accepting money for a referral will diminish your credibility. Refer people because they are the best in their field or niche. Because you believe they are the absolute best fit for the party to whom you are referring them and relevant for the current circumstances. If it is a normal practice to accept compensation, then it would be acceptable.

- **Refer only people you know, like and trust.** It is essential that you apply all three of these criteria. Your network is full of qualified resources. Refer the best!

- **Give more than you receive.** Just as a fully functioning network relies on the giving and receiving of all parties to remain dynamic, so does the world of referrals. Focus on giving more referrals than you receive. The benefits of your efforts will materialize in the form of quality referrals tailor made for you.

- **Send a note.** When you make a referral, send a letter, note or email to the people to whom you are referring. Be sure to send a copy to the professional whom you are referring and include:

  - Your name and contact information
  - The name and contact information of the professional being referred
  - Details of the client needs and circumstances

- **Help others refer you.** Giving more referrals than receiving them does not mean you shouldn't help others in your network refer you effectively. The two best things you can do are to provide your contacts with:

  - A written script your contacts can use when they refer you to others
  - A profile of what an ideal client or referral for you would be – what type of business or person you would like. If you don't know what type of referral you are looking for, you probably won't find it. Identify your ideal referral and then share the information with your contacts.

Following these tips will make a world of difference in your referral process and in the growing effectiveness of your networks.

2. Send handwritten notes.

This second technique for working your networks will add a personal touch to your networking interactions.

Technology has had an amazing effect on communications. With email and instant messaging, you can contact someone in a matter of seconds. Although this is very convenient, it is impersonal when it comes to expressing a personal sentiment – whether you want to express your gratitude or just let someone know you are thinking of them.

If you want to make a special impression, stand out from the crowd and strengthen your personal connection with someone, sending a personal, handwritten note will be far more effective. A handwritten note allows you to convey feelings and nurture a relationship in a way that digital communications cannot. If you think about it, the days of handwritten letters are long gone. Few people take the time. Handwritten correspondence is a dying form of communication. Consider the following:

- When most people go through their mail, the first pieces they open are envelopes with a stamp that are hand-addressed versus those that have printed addresses and metered postage. It is human nature for people to be excited by the receipt of a personal card or invitation. The typical household receives an onslaught of "junk mail" and the handwritten note will usually be opened first!

- People tend to save handwritten cards and display them for some time. These displays are evidence that someone else cares about them and they evoke positive feelings. They have staying power and keep your image alive.

- Handwritten notes show that you care. The recipient knows you took time from your busy day to think about them and to pay special attention to them.

So, assuming you are convinced of the value of taking the time to send handwritten notes, here are some tips for when and how to send handwritten note cards in a manner which increases your networking effectiveness:

■ Identify target recipients.

Start by going through your database, identifying people whom you may have neglected or to whom you owe a thank you. Next, look at each contact and identify those people who have helped you the most. Send them a card to express how much they mean to you.

■ Make note writing a daily habit.

Once you have caught up by sending notes to your targeted contacts, establish the habit of sending cards to people every day. Start small with two or three cards per day. Each week, increase the number of cards you write. Aim for ten notes a day, or more, if you can and be sure to make a note in your database each time you send a handwritten note.

■ Look for interesting cards.

Always be on the lookout for intriguing and appropriate cards. Get into the habit of picking up interesting cards during your travels. Look for cards that express who you are, what you believe in and the image you want to project. These cards will remind people about the qualities you want them to remember when they think of you.

Also, look for cards that highlight places, activities or interests, which are important to your contacts. These cards will let people know you take a real interest in them. For example, if you have contacts who love to golf, purchase some cards featuring beautiful golf courses.

You can also have custom cards made with your business name, logo and branding, although these cards convey more of a marketing statement than a personal message. For that reason, I recommend you save those for more formal communications and, instead, look for cards which provide a personal reflection of you and your relationship with the person receiving the card.

■ Keep cards handy.

Keep a stack of cards on your desk as a constant reminder. Also, keep plenty of note cards at home, as well as in your car, briefcase and luggage when you travel. You never know when someone will do something which deserves a handwritten note. Always have cards within reach so you can write a note as soon as the thought strikes you.

■ Highlight people's special interests.

When you write a note, be sure to review the recipient's contact information so you can make reference to any special interests, projects and family members which are unique to them. This shows your clients you care about them and they are important enough for you to remember details about their lives. It is these very details which will separate you from the crowd and highlight the importance of keeping enough data on each client.

- **Include items of interest.**

Again, using the personal information in your database, consider adding press clippings or articles of interest as enclosures with the note card. For example, I have a contact who is an avid fly fisherman. When I come across an article or magazine piece on the subject, I clip it and send it with a note saying. "I remembered you enjoy fly fishing and thought you might find this interesting." Once you get in the habit of doing this, your mind will be trained to always be on the lookout for these items of interest.

- **Look for reasons to send cards.**

Some typical reasons to send a note card are to:

- Say thank you and recognize great service or a kind gesture
- Acknowledge anyone who helped make your day better
- Say thank you to a prospective client from whom you did *not* get business. If things do not work out with the person they selected, they will probably remember your kind note and return to you.
- Congratulate people who have made accomplishments in their career. Remember, scan the local newspapers and business journals to watch for mention of people who are "on the move."

Many, many reasons exist for sending handwritten note cards. We have included a list of possible reasons and favorite interests in Figure 5-1. Look it over and see which ideas may inspire you to send some note cards today.

Whatever the reason, a handwritten note, on an interesting card, with a nice ink pen, will make your contacts feel special and strengthen your personal connection with them.

Once you start the process of sending cards and making it part of your day, you will not believe the impact it will have on you and your networks. For me, the best and most unexpected part of this process is the number of cards I started to receive back from people. I am so fortunate to be able to start my day by reading cards from the people in my life who are most important to me. It, once again, reinforces our major premise: the more you give, the more you will receive.

Figure 5-1: Ideas for Sending Note Cards		
Reasons to Send Note Cards		**Favorite Themes**
Thank you for …	To send a clipping	Foods
Providing help	Accomplishment	Restaurants
Making a difference	Holiday	Colors
Advice	Birthday	Hobbies
Appreciation	Anniversary	Sports
Understanding	Wedding	Travel destinations
Great service	Engagement	Vacation spots
Encouragement	Gradation	Clubs or groups
Remembering	New baby	Associations
Speaking with you	Get well	Music
A great idea	Condolences	Pets
Taking time	Any special occasion	Movies or theater
Calling	No occasion at all	Television shows
Catching up		Arts
Just because		Flowers
You were on my mind		Cars
I saw & thought of you		Mentors/heroes
These are just a few ideas. Add your own. Any reason, or no special reason at all, provides a good time to send a handwritten note card.		

3. Implement the "Daily Datum."

The third technique for working your network is to establish a pattern of simple daily actions that will greatly improve the effectiveness of your networks, your business and your life.

When implementing a new project, motivation and the excitement of the new venture get you started. Over time, however, it is the habits you develop which keep you going.

Many experts have proclaimed the value of developing positive habits leading to success:

Steven Covey, author of "Seven Habits Of Highly Effective People" and numerous other books, wrote, "Our character is basically a composite of our habits. Because they are consistent, often unconscious patterns, they constantly, daily, express our character."

Brian Tracy, well-known Canadian leadership consultant and author, said, "Successful people are simply those with successful habits."

Confucius, the ancient philosopher is attributed with the saying, "Men's natures are alike; it is their habits that separate them."

The point is, developing good habits will surely help you embrace new behaviors, leading to positive results. Our habits will determine who we are and that will determine the degree of success which flows around us.

Now anyone who has tried to alter their behavior by developing new habits knows change does not come easily. Too often, change and improvement are viewed as a very difficult process. It makes sense. Looking at the gap between where you are and where you want to be can be intimidating. Estimating the time it may take to devote new habits can be discouraging.

The best way to develop new habits is to break those desired new behaviors into small, discrete steps, which are not too overwhelming. Breaking the new behaviors down into small practices, performed consistently, provides the path to best results and is precisely why I developed the Daily Datum.

The **Daily Datum** is a recommended plan of simple tasks to be completed each day for 20 minutes. For each day, Monday through Friday, just complete the corresponding task. The five tasks are easy and take only 20 minutes a day. Repeat each task on its associated day of the week for the next 90 days, at which point you will start to see improvements in your business and networks. Here they are:

Monday – Handwritten Notes

You already know the importance of this activity, so why not start your week with writing notes on Monday? Take 20 minutes to write handwritten notes to anyone in your network. Use the notes to express gratitude, reconnect, pass along some information or express your feelings about someone or something.

Tuesday – Phone Calls

Each Tuesday, call several people in your database. Have a chat with each one for about five minutes. Contact people you have lost touch with, haven't spoken to for a while, or past clients or customers. Do not call people in your inner circle, those you communicate with on a regular basis. Reach out to those you don't normally see. Be sure to enter the date you spoke to the contact in your database. This way, you will be able to track how frequently you speak. Finally, and most importantly, end each phone conversation with one of the following phrases:

"Please let me know if there is anything I can do for you"
"Please let me know if I can help you in any way"

We will talk more about this at the end of the chapter. For now, make a mental note to end each conversation this way.

Wednesday – Database Maintenance

Every Wednesday, spend about 20 minutes going into your database and to do some housekeeping. Review your contact records and make sure that each contact is rated, using the "A-B-C-D Method" described in Step One. Then, add any updated information about the contact. Maintaining a database of 250 contacts or more can be a daunting task. If you work on it for 20 minutes a day, one day a week, you will have it in tip-top shape in no time and it will not feel like such an excruciating task.

Thursday – Network Development

Each Thursday, spend your 20 minutes meeting someone new or taking an action that will add a new member to your network database. If you meet new people face-to-face, be sure to get their contact information and follow up with handwritten notes. In Step Six, we will talk more about ways to recruit new contacts and grow your networks. For now, just know Thursday is the day you will put those techniques to work.

Friday – Helping Others

You made it to the end of the week, but you are not done yet. Every Friday, for 20 minutes, I want you to use your expertise to help someone else who needs it. This can come in the form of direct assistance to a coworker or by mentoring someone else in the form of a 20-minute phone call each week.

It is the responsibility of all strong leaders to pass down the skills and information they have acquired to others. This is your opportunity to do just that – to add value to the lives of others.

Congratulations! Now you have made it through the week and I want to reinforce why doing all of these things consistently each week is so valuable to your growth and success.

Too often, as we work to advance our careers and businesses, we tend to spend the bulk of our development time concentrating on ourselves – improving our knowledge and skills, attending training seminars and conferences, advertising and marketing our businesses and ourselves.

During my career, I have found repeatedly that the fastest path to success was through adopting these two philosophies:

- As you reach up to grab the next rung of the ladder, make sure you reach down to pull someone else up along the way.
- Remember, every time you give to others, you will receive something of equal or greater value back tenfold. It is what I call the Giver's Gain.

As you adopt this mindset and complete the tasks in the Daily Datum on a regular and consistent basis, you will start to see a change in the way you are viewed by others and in your business as well.

4. Nurture your inner circle.

While the Daily Datum focused more on bringing new people into your networks and staying in touch with those with whom you do not communicate with regularly, the fourth technique focuses on your inner circle, the people you are closest and with whom you have the deepest relationships.

If you wish to be truly effective and add value to the lives of others, you will find you cannot do it alone. If it takes a village to raise a child, it certainly takes a network to succeed in business.

Your village, or network, starts with your inner circle, which is where I want you to focus now. Start by making a list of the people to whom you are closest, including:

- Family members
- Trusted advisors
- Mentors
- Close friends
- Spiritual leaders

These are the people who go beyond contacts or members of a network. They are, in essence, the fabric of your life.

Once you have your list, I want you to review it and, as you go through it, identify two categories of people: mentors and trusted advisors.

Mentors

A mentor is a wise and trusted counselor or teacher, someone who provides guidance. If you have ever had or been a mentor, you know it can be a wonderful experience. It is a gift for both individuals and offers support at its highest form.

Mentors can come in a variety of types and for many reasons. They can be work-related, personal, spiritual or even sports-based. Whatever the area of focus, the person has significantly more experience and insight on the particular topics on which you seek counsel. Mentors tend to be older and their wisdom comes from their life experiences. They have been where you are and are where you want to be. Although, the age difference is not always true. Sometimes, a person who is younger may serve as a mentor because of their knowledge and expertise in a special area.

As you review your network contacts, identify individuals who serve as mentors in particular areas of your life and those with whom you may play the role of mentor. By passing along this gift, you keep the art of mentoring alive and pay forward the wonderful experience you yourself have been privileged to enjoy.

Trusted Advisors

Trusted advisors come in two major categories:

(1) Those who offer expert advice on a particular subject, situation or business problem

(2) Those who are life advisors.

For specific advice, you may want several people in your camp. These people are sometimes referred to as Mavens or Subject Matter Experts in a particular field or practice.

For general life advice, you may turn to a family member, a spiritual or religious advisor or close friend.

In either case, the key to the success of these relationships begins with the willingness of both parties to be open and honest with one another. With that also comes discretion and confidentiality.

With these guidelines in mind, take some time to go through your list of contacts and identify those whom you believe are, or might be, candidates to serve as mentors and/or trusted advisors.

Your Personal Advisory Board

Now that you have identified individuals whom you consider your inner circle, including your mentors and trusted advisors, I am going to recommend you form your own personal advisory board.

Your personal advisory board is a small select group of people whom you can trust to be honest with you and whom you can go to for help and advice in times of need.

In many situations in life, we are reluctant to share our dreams, goals and ideas with others. When we do find the courage or comfort level to share this information with others, they often respond by telling us what they think we want to hear rather than being objective and giving us honest feedback. This is not their fault. It is a pre-programmed response by most people who want to be supportive. For an advisory board to be truly useful, you need to hear the good, the bad and sometimes the ugly.

For your personal advisory board, choose individuals who can serve as a true sounding board; provide honest observations and guidance. Learning the truth from your personal advisory board will save you time, prevent you from making poor decisions and keep you from going down the wrong path.

With this in mind, here are a few characteristics to consider when selecting members of your advisory board:

- **Honesty and candor.** The truth can hurt sometimes, but never as badly as making the wrong decision

- **Accountability.** Choose people who will hold you accountable. By having people to whom you are accountable outside your normal work and family situations, you will find the ability to accomplish more in a shorter period of time. Take goals, for example. If you write your goals down and share them with your personal advisory board, you will be much more likely to accomplish them.

- **Comfort Level.** Your board should consist of people with whom you can feel comfortable letting your guard down. For your personal advisory board to be truly effective, it should consist of people with whom you are willing to share all of your thoughts and feelings with openness and honesty.

You are now armed with several powerful techniques, which will enable you to work your networks effectively. If you make it a regular practice to make referrals, send handwritten notes, follow the Daily Datum, and nurture and utilize your inner circle, you will find your life will start to change in very positive ways.

Please let me know...

Before we leave the topic of how to work your networks effectively, I want to return to one concept I mentioned earlier – ending every conversation with an offer to help.

Two of the most common questions I am asked when it comes to working within a network are:

- How do I ask for the assistance of others without looking like I am on the take?

- How do I help others without looking like I have a hidden agenda?

The answer to both is the same: Sincerity shows and transcends these thoughts. When you are consistent, honest and sincere, others will recognize it and they will not harbor thoughts about scorekeeping and hidden agendas.

Over time, I have found that one of the best ways to develop and demonstrate this sincerity is to get in the habit of ending every conversation – whether face-to-face, by telephone, or email – with one of two phrases:

"Please let me know if there is anything I can do for you"
"Please let me know if I can help you in any way"

You cannot just ask the question. You have to mean it.

When someone does request your help or assistance, stop what you are doing, write it down and take action on it as soon as possible. By asking and not following through, you will do more damage than if you had just kept quiet in the first place.

Once this becomes habit, the trust and faith people have in you will multiply. The people in my life are so used to me saying this now that they anticipate it. Often, they will see me and say, "Nothing today, Larry." It always comes with a smile on their face and in their voice and I love it!

In addition, I think you will find that people will not abuse your good intentions. When they do ask for something, it is usually important to them. When the day comes that you need a favor from them, they will be there for you.

It may take a little time to develop this level of sincerity and trust. Interestingly, when you first reach out to people with genuine care and concern, do not be surprised if they shy away. So many people are used to being taken advantage of and mistreated. They may be leery of your true intentions at first. Don't worry. Just keep reaching out. The tide will change.

Eventually, you will find this simple offer of help, along with the four techniques described in this chapter, will enable you to bring your networks alive and build true Social Capital. Even if your network of contacts is small, it will be powerful. It will be a network of high quality contacts because you have been working on deepening your relationships. That is what networking in the Relationship Age is all about.

STEP SIX:
IMPROVE YOUR NETWORKS

*"Talents are best nurtured in solitude, but character
is best formed in the stormy billows of the world."*
~ Johann Wolfgang von Goethe

Taking the daily actions and pursuing the simple habits described in the previous chapter will keep your networks humming along smoothly and effectively. Still, you should always be on the lookout for new and fresh ways to improve the quality and quantity of your networks.

Bigger and better networks produce bigger and better results. You should always strive to improve the number and quality of contacts in your networks. Step Six – Improve Your Networks - is a simple process and involves three techniques:

1. Recruit new contacts.
2. Update and upgrade your contacts.
3. Stay connected with all contacts.

Let's look at each technique individually.

1. Recruit new contacts.

For a network to stay intact and relevant to your current situation, you always have to be adding to it. If left unattended, for any length of time, the number of contacts in your network will begin to dwindle. People move, pass away and leave for a variety of reasons. To balance this attrition, you must make regular efforts to meet new people and add them to your networks. Just think, if you meet only one new person per week, that's 52 new people per year to add to your network.

In this day and age, there are many places to meet new people. Figure 6-1 includes some ideas and here are some of the most effective places to meet new contacts:

- **Business Gatherings.** Whether you attend those organized by others or host your own, business mixers and get-togethers are a perfect place to meet new business contacts. Many local chambers of commerce, associations and professional networking groups hold monthly events specifically to allow business professionals to exchange leads on a regular basis. You may also wish to join a professional networking group organized for the sole purpose of exchanging leads.

  Do not hesitate to reach out yourself and take other business owners to lunch. Go through your database and pick someone to invite to lunch. Ask them to bring along a guest you don't know. Similarly, choose people from your database who don't know each other and take them to lunch together. This will help you meet new contacts and deepen your relationships with existing contacts.

  Also, read your local newspaper and business trade publications for announcements of special events you can attend and people you may wish to contact.

- **Social Gatherings.** Get out and attend as many events as possible, especially those most likely to attract people who are different from your normal spheres of activity and circles of friends. Yes, you are tired at the end of the day, but attending social events can be invigorating to you as well as to your networks. If possible, arrive early so you can spend time with the host and greet other guests as they arrive. They will appreciate your kindness in making them feel comfortable.

Figure 6-1: Places to Meet New Contacts	
■ Business mixers	■ Cultural and art groups and events
■ Social gatherings	■ Volunteer work
■ Seminars and workshops	■ Chamber of commerce gatherings
■ Trade Shows	■ School alumni groups
■ Non-profit and charity events	■ Parent Teacher Association events
■ Political group meetings	■ Parents groups
■ Sports and recreational events	■ On-line social networks
■ Civic Organization	

- **Conferences, Trade Shows and Educational Seminars.** Professional conferences and educational seminars offer an excellent opportunity to make new contacts in your field of interest. If you keep your eyes and ears open, you can meet Subject Matter Experts, movers, shakers and pioneers relevant in your field. After seminars, seek out the speaker and other knowledgeable people in the room. Introduce yourself, inquire about them and the work they are doing. Ask for their business cards, add their information to your database and follow up immediately.

If you go to your industry's major conference or trade show regularly, you probably run into the same people each time. This is a great opportunity to reconnect but, for a change of pace, you may want to consider going to trade shows in other related industries where you can find a niche and meet new people.

- **In Transit.** An excellent time to meet people is when you are on the move. Whether you are on a plane across country or mass transit across town, meeting new contacts in the larger public sphere can be quite rewarding. Respect people's space, but be alert to opportunities. For example, I once saw a celebrated author in an airport. I went over, introduced myself, acknowledged my familiarity with his work and thanked him. I gave him my business card and, a few years later, I was invited to participate in a special program he offers. People like to be recognized. You never know what might happen or what a brief conversation might lead to if you don't reach out.

- **Social Media Websites.** As more and more people participate in social media networks, they are adding new and different opportunities for meeting people. Many sites offer the capability of posting announcements of specific events in local areas, online webinars and other venues for meeting, conversing with and developing relationships with new people. This is an ideal way to use Social Media Websites. Remember, finding new contacts is just the first step. You still must add them to your own database, collect information on them and develop a relationship.

Tips for Meeting New Contacts

Now that you have some places in mind where you can meet new contacts to add to your database, I would like to share a few tips which have helped me be successful in that first contact. Meeting and greeting people for the first time is not something that comes naturally to everyone. The strategies below have helped me and many of the people I have worked with immensely:

- **Prepare.** Before you go to any event, whether it is a networking, social, seminar or trade show, take time to do your homework. If it is a new event, answer these questions:
    - What is the ultimate purpose of the event?
    - Who is responsible for organizing and funding the event?
    - Who normally attends the event?
    - How long and how often is it held?
    - Who are the sponsors of the event?

You should always strive to be as well-versed as possible about an event before you arrive. By knowing who the key players are, you will know who to thank and acknowledge when you meet them. It also serves as a good conversation starter if you are shy. If you don't get a chance to meet the event organizers, it's always a good idea to send a thank you card the next day.

- **Introduce people.** One of the best ways to expand your network is to assist other people in meeting one another. Be a Connector who brings other people together. Be the person others can count on to make the introduction or refer them to someone who can help solve their problems or address their needs. Once again, arrive early and don't be a shy wallflower. One method I use to make it easier is to pretend the event is my own. I try to greet guests as they enter. Most people are nervous about breaking the ice. If you do this, others will be very grateful.

- **Ask open-ended questions.** When you are speaking with someone new, ask open-ended questions, questions which cannot be answered with a simple yes or no. It sounds simple enough, but when the time arrives, you would be surprised how many people revert to closed questions which don't encourage continued dialogue. Here are a few suggestions:

  - What do you do for a living?
  - Where do you see your industry going in the next few years?
  - What are the biggest problems you face in your business? (This is a great question to ask when you are looking for ways to add value and provides service to the other party.)
  - If you could do anything, would it be your current profession or would you do something else?

- **Listen for referral opportunities.** By seeking to provide value and help others, you will not only meet more people but will also be in a position to refer them to others in your network. I suggest you practice listening for referral opportunities like, "I am looking for a good (fill in the blank)." Or, "Does anyone know a good (fill in the blank)?" These questions are direct requests for referrals.

- **Focus on real connections.** I have always gone to an event with the goal of meeting as many people as I can and establishing a real connection with just a few. We have all met the overly aggressive networker who rushes around an event touting a product or service and pushing business cards into everyone's hands. This behavior is offensive and gives networking a bad name because of the image it leaves in people's minds. It is not effective networking because it does not focus on establishing a relationship. Instead, when you go to a networking event, you will want to meet and greet as many people as you can without being rude, while looking for those people with whom you have a real connection. Once you start chatting with someone, you usually know within a few minutes if you click. If you do, spend time asking questions and getting to know the person.

  Now you have a great opportunity to ask for their business card. This makes it look like making real connections is why you are there in the first place. Once your conversation is over, take a few minutes in private to make some notes of the highlights of your chat. The next day, send a handwritten note card stating what a pleasure it was to meet them and mention a few details of the conversation. This shows you care enough to write, you paid attention and you care about this young relationship.

- **Make a plan.** When you go to a networking event, think about the event beforehand and set one or more goals which are appropriate for the event. This will greatly increase your chances of success. For example, you might set a business development goal of meeting two people who can introduce you to decision makers who would want to purchase your product or service. On the other hand, if you are working for a nonprofit organization, you might set a goal to identify three new donors who would like to donate to your cause. Sometimes, you may get to an event and find it is not what you expected. You may have to change your intended goals. For example, I once attended a conference with a new business development goal; to obtain leads. When I arrived, I realized the attendees were not my target audience, so I shifted my focus to a professional development goal; to meet three people who possessed the subject matter expertise in the specific topic I was researching.

Whatever the nature of the goals, the important thing is to make them **"SMART"** goals – Specific, Measurable, Achievable, Relevant and Timely. With these goals in your mind, you will have a much clearer picture of the results you are seeking and you will be much more likely to achieve them.

2. Update and upgrade your contacts.

While you are out attending networking events, meeting new contacts and adding them to your database, it is also important to continuously review your database and make changes to keep it current. If you are always adding people to your database and not deleting old records or reviewing the information and ratings, your database will quickly become unwieldy and obsolete. You need to reassess, reclassify and weed out.

Every week, when you do housekeeping on your database, review it for people who should be deleted for one reason or another. Perhaps they have moved away. Or, you made some changes in your business and these individuals need no longer be a part of your networks. Do not delete anyone with whom you may still want to be in touch with. Ask yourself if certain contacts are worth the effort of maintaining a relationship. If the answer is "no," then delete their names and contact information from your records. Remember, you have limited time and you want to spend it on people who are current and active and relevant to your business and your life.

In addition to deleting contacts which are no longer active, you should also review your contact ratings. Whether you are using the A-B-C-D Method or another system, go through all of your contacts periodically and see if their ratings have changed. You may wonder why a contact's rating would change. Once an "A," always an "A." Actually, a variety of factors could lead to a change in a person's role in your life. You could change jobs or careers and, as a result, the ratings you have given may change. Some will become less relevant to your business interests and others will become more relevant. Some may drop away entirely.

The important thing to remember is that your database is dynamic and changing all the time. As people and situations change, so should your database. Take time to reflect these changes and keep it current. Whatever the reason, updating contact records and ratings will improve the quality of your networks by keeping them relevant to your life.

3. Stay connected with all contacts.

As you improve the quantity and quality of your network, it is important to stay connected with all of your contacts and let them know they are still part of your network.

Any time you have a major announcement or change is one good way to do this. Perhaps you have received a promotion, or changed companies or have a new product or service announcement. Be sure to share this information with your contacts. Don't just send out a mass letter or email. Take time to follow up in a more personal way, with a phone call or handwritten note. It may take time to do this, but if you work at it step by step, one person at a time, it will keep you connected with all of your contacts. In addition, remember to end each interaction with one of these two phrases:

"Please let me know if there is anything I can do for you"
"Please let me know if I can help you in any way"

One of the most important keys to long-term success is continuous improvement. Think about the work you have put into developing your networks. The last thing you want is for them to become ineffective over time because of negligence. Do not put yourself in a position of having to start over. Make a commitment to take time to add new contacts, delete old contacts, review and upgrade existing contacts and stay connected. This small amount of time spent will be well worth the effort. Continuous improvements to your networks will lead to continuous improvements in your life.

STEP SEVEN:
MAXIMIZE YOUR NETWORKS

"Don't wait for your ship to come in; swim out to it."
~ Jonathan Winters

One of the most important principles for success is the habit of going the extra mile. Marathon winners win by inches. Olympic gold medal winners are fractions of seconds ahead of those who go home with no medals. Business leaders win the deal by offering the smallest extra service. Time and time again, the difference between those who achieve their goals consistently and those who spend their lives and careers merely following others is that extra mile, extra second, or just a tiny bit of extra effort.

Applying this philosophy to networking, I recommend you take care to never become complacent or content with simply performing the everyday tasks of working your networks and improving the quality and quantity of your contacts. Yes, those steps are essential but do not stop there. Go the extra mile and be creative about what you can do to distinguish yourself from the competition, to "stand out" from the crowd. Always ask yourself, "How can I give people more than they expect?"

Step Seven – Maximize Your Network - addresses this question and shares four techniques I have found very successful:

1. Join a professional networking group.
2. Form alliances and "Circles of Endorsements."
3. Embrace what I call the "Four Pillars of Success."
4. Create your own ideas!

1. Join a professional networking group.

One of the most productive actions you can take to maximize your networks is by joining a professional networking group.

A professional networking group is one that is typically formed through an organization specifically dedicated to assisting business owners and sales professionals in building solid and lasting referral business. As a member, you join one specific group which meets on a regular basis to generate quality client referrals for one another. These groups or teams are made up of one professional from each major business field. This eliminates competition among members and creates mutually beneficial business relationships.

Professional networking groups can offer a variety of features that increase their value, including:

- Weekly meetings
- Expert speakers
- Newsletters and electronic communications that present topical business issues, networking tips and referral business strategies
- Educational seminars and workshops
- Special proprietary processes and tools, including software that makes your network management easier and more effective

- Online resources like your own web pages, website links, referral forms, text messages with referral alerts and more

The benefits are significant. Participating in a formal network group will help you to:

- **Expand your networks** – learn from your team members about new people to add to your network contacts.

- **Give & receive quality referrals** – enjoy a consistent flow of qualified referrals from your team members who are dedicated to helping you find new clients.

- **Benefit from a support team** – get the support you need to stay positive through difficult economic times. Give and receive mutual encouragement.

- **Mastermind the power of the team** – coordinate knowledge and effort, in a spirit of harmony, among your group members to address topical business issues. Keep current on the latest opportunities and trends and attain a definite purpose.

Membership and active participation in an active networking group can increase your sales force (without increasing your payroll) and attracts new clients without expensive marketing and advertising. For more, follow these techniques:

2. Form alliances and "Cross Endorsements:"

Another extremely effective method for exponentially increasing your outreach is to form strategic alliances and Cross Endorsements.

The goal is to find a business or profession that is complementary to yours or runs in conjunction with yours, yet is not competitive. Examples include a realtor and mortgage broker, a printer and paper supplier, a landscape designer and garden supply business, a writer and graphic artist, as well as, a computer store and technology consultant. The list is endless! So many opportunities exist for forming strategic alliances in which you will work together and cross endorse each other's products and services.

Once you have formed an alliance with one or several people, you can take advantage of the synergy in a variety of ways:

- **Joint advertising.** The cost of advertising continues to climb each year. If you find others to advertise with, you can share the costs, save money and open up new markets for each other.

- **Written endorsements and testimonials.** As you work with each other, you will be able to provide each other with written endorsements which will be used in sales letters, print media and multimedia like websites and electronic communications.

- **Shared client lists and databases.** When you have established a trusted relationship, you may want to consider making your database and mailing lists available to each other. Since you are in non-competing businesses, loss of customers is not an issue. You can gain clients and establish an agreement to protect the confidentiality of your clients.

- **Co-host seminars and educational events.** This is an outstanding way to build new clients since you will each be bringing a different perspective to the program. Be creative, identify what information your clients need which either of you can provide or design a seminar addressing those needs.

- **Blog together.** Writing a blog is a great way to share information, but can be a daunting task. Having one or several contributing editors will take some of the load off you and also add a different perspective to spice up the blog for your readers.

- **Write for each other's newsletters.** As with blogs, a different perspective is a welcome addition to print newsletters. You can also offer each other a small block ad in your newsletters.

- **Link to each other's websites.** The more links you have to active websites, the better your search engine placements.

The list of ways you can work together will be as long as your imagination will take you. By having solid and trusting relationships with people in complimentary businesses, you can help each other in significant ways.

The Circle of Endorsement

Taking the concept of Cross Endorsements one-step farther, you can create the Circle of Endorsement, which is a group of several businesses, all of which have something to offer one another.

One of the classic circles I have employed is the **"Financial 5"**:

- Stockbroker
- Insurance Broker
- Real Estate Broker
- Loan Broker
- CPA

These five professions are in a perfect position to help one another. To expand more, you might add attorneys who specialize in financial-based businesses.

For yourself, try to pick 3 or more fields related to yours, which are all in a position to help each other.

Many Fortune 500 firms actually establish circles of endorsement under one roof, supplying many different related services, which were once separate businesses. Each center operates as a separate division or profit center tied to the overall corporation.

As an independent contractor or small business, you can achieve the same result and compete against larger firms. In many ways, a tightly aligned cluster of small businesses can provide a higher quality of service to clients than a larger company because each individual business is handling their specialty without conflict of interest with the other divisions or headquarters.

Figure 7-1, at the end of this chapter, includes a comprehensive list of professions to consider when putting together circles of endorsement. Be creative and look for interesting alliances.

Your circle will include as few as three professions or as many as you wish. My own experience is that it is best to not let it get too big. Once a circle gets to eight or more professions, it will become difficult to coordinate and lose its intended effect.

Building a circle of endorsement takes time and trust, but it can result in enormous value to everyone.

3. Embrace the Four Pillars of Success.

Many studies have attempted to identify factors that contribute to success – qualities or traits successful people from different fields have in common. Among those who participated in the studies were business professionals, athletes, celebrated individuals in the arts, science, medicine, politics and many other fields. As it turns out, all of these successful people share some, if not all, of the following **Four Pillars of Success**:

Pillar One: Outstanding Networks – The most successful people all have deep and vast networks. It did not happen by accident. They nurtured and developed their networks over the length of their careers and understand the principle of giving with an expectation of nothing in return.

Pillar Two: Coaches and Mentors – We have also seen that they did not rise to the top alone. Most highly effective and successful people have had or still have outstanding coaches. They seek the best in class for what they are trying to accomplish and learn from them. Mentorship plays a big role as well. Not only do they have people mentor them along the way but they act as mentors to others as well.

Pillar Three: A Niche – In most cases, these highly successful people have a deep niche they serve. By having a niche, they were able to eliminate a lot of competition, and they were able to become a household name in their particular area of expertise. If you look at the top people in most fields, they are not necessarily the very best in what they do, but they are perceived to be the best by the public because they built their niche before anyone else.

Pillar Four: A Mastermind Group – Another important element on the rise to the top was participation in a mastermind group. Not only does such a group enable you to harness the power of a team and apply it toward specific goals, but it provides a diverse and balanced sounding board that proves to be invaluable, especially in business. Having an honest sounding board of whom you can try ideas before taking them public can prevent you from making costly mistakes.

These Four Pllars of Success will ensure a solid structure; provide the support you need to pursue diverse new activities and contacts which will place you among the successful leaders.

Additional analysis of highly successful people indicates they approach their business and life with the following traits:

1. They are VERY clear on their goals, intentions and desired accomplishments.

2. Once clear in their own mind, they develop a deep belief system in their goals and gain unstoppable energy.

3. They ignore the naysayers. If they hit a wall, they go around, below or above it, but they will not be stopped.

What is stopping you from achieving your dreams? You, too, can apply these Four Pillars of Success and adopt qualities which will lead to your success.

4. Create your own ideas!

After getting to this point, you are now full of ideas on how to develop, work, improve and maximize your networks to great success. Here is one last idea – create your own ideas!

Yes, you will always find great ideas from other resources – from networking groups, books, websites and your contacts. However, the best ideas may come out of your very own experiences.

Who else knows you better? Understands your situation better? Embraces your dreams more? Creativity is a funny thing and sometimes people can come up with great ideas at the most unexpected times. They don't have to be anything earth shattering – sometimes the simplest ideas work best. The point is to let yourself be creative. Here are a few simple ideas I have created and which others have shared:

- **Index Cards** – After being caught off guard at events where I wanted to make notes on someone I had just met, I came up with the idea of carrying 3" x 5" index cards with me. They are small enough to carry and just the right size for making notes. Obviously, it is no technologically advanced brainstorm, but I tried it and it works perfectly. You never catch me without an index card. I never miss jotting information on an important new contact when I meet them.

- **Business & Legal Sections** – An insurance agent once shared the idea of going through the business section of the local newspaper and look for people who were recently promoted or hired into new, notable jobs. On that occasion, you could contact them. I found it to be a great idea. One day, while going through the paper, I happened to glance at the legal section, which included "fictitious business name" announcements of new businesses. That was another good source of contacts I found. I have used both of these ideas; which have added numerous contacts to my networks.

- **Project Teams** – Whenever I have a goal or project, I look through my database to see who has expertise in that area and who might be able to assist me. One time, I found several people and I was having a hard time deciding which person to contact. Suddenly it dawned on me that I didn't have to limit myself to one person. I could form a team. This is especially beneficial on larger projects.

- **Visualization** – This is a concept I had read about, but it didn't really register, until one day when I was trying to figure out how to improve my sales. This may sound a bit ethereal, but I decided to start visualizing the success I really desired. I would visualize myself receiving the highest sales award possible – being called up to the front of the room at a special event to receive it in front of my peers. Every day, I visualized this event and… Yes, it happened. A few years later, when I moved into management, I would visualize meetings the night before, running through them in my mind – how I wanted them to go, what the desired outcome would be. It was like a dress rehearsal which made the actual meetings so much more effective.

These are all simple examples, although their effect on my productivity and success was enormous.

We get ideas and suggestions multiple times throughout the day and often we do not realize how important they are. They seem like small matters at the time, but the impact on our lives can be quite consequential. They can truly maximize our networking effectiveness.

Figure 7-1: Circle of Endorsement List of Professions

Accountant – CPA	Auto Body	Career Coaching
Access Control	Auto Sales – Leasing	Carpet – Upholstery Cleaner
Actuaries	Auto Repair	Casting Agency
Acupuncture	Baby Sitting	Catalogs
Acupuncture	Baby Products	Caterer
Adjusters	Bags	Cellular Phones
Adoption Services	Bail Bonds	Chiropractor
Adult Care Facilities	Bands	Cleaning Services Residential – Commercial
Adult Education	Banker	Cement
Advertising Agency	Bars	Cemetery – Funeral
Advertising Specialty	Barber	Chartering
Agriculture	Bartender	Check Cashing
Airlines	Bathroom Fixtures	Chemical Companies
Aircraft	Batteries	Child Care
Air Ducts	Bearings	Churches – Temple
Air Filter	Beauty School	Children's Businesses
Alarm Systems	Beauty Products	Clothing Business
Alcohol	Bed and Breakfast	Coffee Business
Ambulance Service	Bedding	Collection Agency
Amusement	Beverage Supply	Comics
Answering Service	Billboard Advertising	Comedian
Antiques	Bill Pay Service	Communication
Appliances	Blueprinting	Consulting
Arborist	Boating Sales	Computer Sales
Aquariums	Boat Repair	Computer Hardware
Arial Photography	Body Guard	Computer Software
Architect	Bookkeeping	Computer Programmer
Archaeologist	Book Sales	Computer Networking
Artist	Booking Agents	Concrete
Art Business	Bricklayer	Construction
Art Gallery	Breeder	Contractor – General
Assisted Living	Builder	Cooking Supply
Astronomy	Business Consultant	Cosmetics
Attorney – Family Law	Business Coach	Counselors
Attorney – Trust, Estate	Business Equipment	Convention and Meeting
Attorney - Real Estate, Contracts, Business	Cabinets	Country Clubs
Audio – Visual Technician	Calibration Service	Coupon Advertising
Audiologist	Camera and Video	Crating Service
Auditor	Camping	Credit Repair
	Candy	

Figure 7-1: Circle of Endorsement List of Professions

Credit Unions	Fire Protection	Interior Design
Crime Fighting Police	Finance Companies	Internet Marketing
Data Cabling	Financial Planner	Internet Service Provider
Data Networks	Fish	Investments
Dating Service - Matchmakers	Flooring – Carpets	Jewelry
	Florist	Landscaping
Data Processor	Food Business	Laboratories
Data Storage	Framing	Lasers
Data Security	Franchising	Learning Service
Day Spa	Freight	Legal Services
Decorator	Fundraisers	Lighting Companies
Dentist	Furniture	Limousines
Designers	Garbage Removal – Recycling	Liquidator – Auctions
Detectives		Liquor
Diet Business	Gardener – Landscape	Lumber - Hardware
Digital Photo – Video	Gift Baskets	Long Distance Telephony
Direct Mail	Gift Stores	Management Consultant
DJ	Glass Business	Magazines
Doctors	GPS	Mailing Companies
Document Imaging	Gym – Equipment	Marine Services
Drilling	Graphic Artist	Masonry
Driving School	Handicap Services	Marketing Consultant
Drivers	Hardware Store	Marketing Management
Electrician	Hair Stylist	Marketing Sales
Engineering	Health Club	Massage Therapist
Engines	Health Care	Medical Supply
Entertainment Business	Health Insurance	Meeting Planners
Environmental Control	Herbalist	Merchant Services – Credit Cards
Estate Planning	Heating – Cooling Contractor	Metals
Estate Liquidation		Microwave
Equipment Leasing	Hospitals	Mobile Homes
Event Planner	Hypnosis	Model Makers
Excavation	Imaging	Models
Eye Care	Inspectors	Motivational Services
Facial Care	Insect Control	Motor Homes
Family Planning	Insurance – Commercial Business	Motorcycles
Fashion Consulting		Mortgage Broker – Banker
Fencing	Insurance – Home Residential	Moving Companies
Film	Insurance Auto	Multimedia Promotions
Filters	Insurance Life	

Figure 7-1: Circle of Endorsement List of Professions

Music	Property Management	Surveyor
Nail Salons	Psychotherapist	Surgeon
News Services	Public Relations	Surveillance
Newspapers	Publishers	Swimming Pool
Night Clubs	Pumps	Tailors
Nurses	Radio Advertising	Talent Agents
Novelties	Real Estate Appraiser	Tattooing
Nutritional	Real Estate Commercial	Telecommunication
Office Cleaning	Real Estate Residential	Television Advertising
Office Produce – Supply	Real Estate Rental	Theatrical
Organizers	Relocation Company	Tires
Optometrist	Roofers	Tour Guides
Packing Supply	Restaurants	Tool Makers - Sales
Packers	Retirement Businesses	Technical Writer
Painters	Sales Training	Technology Consulting
Paper Business	Sales Management	Telecommunications
Parking Services	Scanning – Copies	Telemarketing
Paralegals	Scientific	Telephone Systems
Personal Assistant	Schools	Temporary Service
Personal Shopper	Security Systems	Trade Show
Personal Chef	Semiconductor	Travel Agents
Personal Coach	Shipping	Trophies and Awards
Personal Trainer	Signs – Banners	Trucking – Shipping
Pest Control	Software Consultant	Typographers
Pets Supply	Software Education	Tutors
Pharmaceuticals	Software Sales	Typing Services
Pharmacy	Special Events	Utilities Audits
Phone Systems	Sporting Goods	Vending
Photographer	Sports Business	Venture Capital
Physical Therapist	Sprinklers	Videographer
Physical Trainer	Stickers	Virtual Assistant
Physician	Stereo Equipment	Volunteers
Piping	Stone Masons	Waste Management
Plastics	Stationary	Warehouses – Storage
Plumber	Stress Management	Web Design
Podiatrist	Stock Broker	Web Hosting
Pottery	Surveyor	Wedding Industry
Pool Companies	Surgeon	Wellness
Preschools	Surveillance	Windows
Printer	Swimming Pool	Wireless
Professional Organizer	Tailors	Word Processing

THE RETURN ON YOUR NETWORKING INVESTMENT

"For it is in giving that we receive."

~ St. Francis of Assisi

After investing a considerable amount of time and energy in applying the steps described in this book, I am sure you are curious how long this process will take to yield results and what you can expect.

In this chapter, we will identify the different kinds of results my Effective Networking Process will produce, when you can expect them and some basic tips for success.

You may recall, at the beginning of this book, I told you I was going to share with you the secrets, which have led to my success. They will transform your life as well. Here is why I am so happy to share these concepts with you – because the more you give, the more amazing the benefits you will receive!

It is a simple concept as old as the ages. Yet, when it comes to networking, it seems to have exponential power. Not in a quid pro quo way, but in an immeasurable way. Sometimes, the results will be anticipated but, at other times, they come as a complete surprise.

Let's look at some examples.

Return in Cost Savings

One of my clients related to me how effective networking saved her thousands of dollars. She had just started a new business and was about to sign a lease for new office space located a few blocks from her apartment building. She was excited and loved that she would be able to walk to work.

A few weeks prior to signing the lease, she was making her normal weekly networking calls and reached out to her apartment manager, with whom she had not spoken for some time. They were having a lively conversation when the apartment manager, who had years of expertise in real property management, offered to look over the commercial lease. It turned out, my client would have been responsible for a tremendous array of expenses she never imagined – including paying a share of the real estate taxes for the property!

My client had assumed commercial leases were pretty much like residential leases where the property owner pays almost all of the expenses. My client averted making a mistake that would have cost her thousands of dollars, thanks to her contact with a real property management Subject Matter Expert who was part of her network.

Return in Professional Achievements

Early in my career, I was working for a residential real estate firm and attended a real estate networking event. An agent I had known for some time introduced me to a Vice President from another firm. I did not give him my card right away, but engaged him in conversation. We ended up have quite a lively conversation about sales and marketing management and I asked for his business card. A week or two later, I came across a marketing book I thought he would enjoy and I sent it to him. I received a nice thank you note. Then, a few months later and totally out of the blue, he called me personally to tell me about a management position that had just opened up. I interviewed and was hired. That's how I moved into management – through networking!

More recently, after I had been working on this book for some time, I took a brief break from work and brought some people from my past – people I had not seen for quite a long time – together for a small dinner party. At the time, I had been totally immersed in the writing process, had a lot of material, but was really in need of a good editor to help me pull it all together for publication. Never in a million years could I have guessed one of my dinner guests – who spent his career as a merchant seafarer – would recommend a highly skilled editor who had the skills I needed. Thanks to my dinner guest, you now have my first book in your hands!

These are two examples of how unexpected the results from networking can be. You never know what surprises it will bring you. The gifts are endless. The value is immeasurable.

Return in Increased Revenues

During difficult economic times, people in all fields are looking for cost-effective ways to attract new clients and increase their business revenues. The traditional ways of print advertising, broadcast media, sales promotion, marketing collateral, telemarketing and direct sales people are all quite costly. Newer methods such as Social Networking are still being tested. Effective networking, on the other hand, is both low in cost and high in productivity.

One of the best examples I can think of is of a young woman who started her own business selling natural herb-scented home decor products. The business was just starting and she wanted to expand her client base and increase sales. She decided to attend the San Francisco Gift Show and seek new opportunities to sell her products. Before she attended, I taught her my concept of the **"Cross Endorsement"**. I advised her to look specifically for another business in a complementary field which would cross endorse her products.

As luck and good networking effort would have it, she found a company which made beautiful greeting cards. The two companies formed a relationship. My associate enclosed a sample greeting card with contact information in every package she sent out. The greeting card company included one of my associate's product catalogs in every package mailed. The results were phenomenal! Within 90 days, both companies experienced a tremendous growth in their customers and sales revenues.

In a far different field, a young technology consultant sought my advice on how to establish a web design and technology consulting business. I taught him my Effective Networking Process and, within a short time of applying the seven steps, he had a highly active consulting business, at only 26 years of age. With networking, increased sales do not have to be costly.

Return in Professional Development

Many years ago, a friend who was a successful marketing consultant, relocated from the east coast to California. She struggled to stay connected with her contacts across the country but continued to send notes and make phone calls. She often wondered if it was worth the effort. Then, one afternoon, she was sitting in her office and the phone rang. The call was from a New York friend whom she had just spoken to a few weeks ago. He was calling from China to invite her to join him in teaching a marketing course to business students at a university in China.

My friend hesitated at what seemed like a huge undertaking, but she decided the experience would be good for her own professional development. She had become so enmeshed in business that she had not been challenged to pursue her own development. The trip turned out to be amazing. My friend met extraordinary people, learned as much as she taught, was awarded an honorary degree from the University where she taught and gained knowledge and skills which have contributed to her success in all kinds of positions and assignments ever since.

We may not all go to China for such a wonderful professional development experience. The good news is we can learn so much in a variety of settings and times. Often, the gatekeepers to those experiences are people in our databases; people who can help us step out of our routines and pursue new challenges resulting in greater success throughout all of our lives.

Return in Relationships

Even when you may not be able to cite results in monetary terms, you will find networking leads to some incredible relationships.

A few days ago, I was speaking to an associate who just returned from a networking event, which included chief executive officers and venture capitalists from around the globe. He said, "Larry, I used your approach and walked away with six new relationships. Not just leads, but people whom I am speaking to on a regular basis. I know these relationships will be mutually beneficial to us all."

My friend went on to relate a very interesting thing about his contacts. He asked them if they had developed any other relationships at the event. They all said no. None of the six had built a relationship with anyone else in the room besides him. They met many people and gave away numerous business cards but none were of great value. Most of the people they met were busy communicating what they were hoping to gain. My friend, on the other hand, was quiet about his own needs and focused on discovering the needs and interests of the people he was engaging in conversation. In fact, he left his own business cards at home. He did ask for their cards, though, and followed up the next day with a handwritten note. A simple step – one that works with even the highest level of professionals.

How Soon Will Results Appear?

The nature and timing of the return on your networking investment will not always be predictable.

You will find some activities show positive results rather quickly. Sending handwritten notes is a good example. Once you get in the habit of writing just a few notes a day, you will start receiving them back in a very short period of time. When someone gets a note from you, they realize you took the time to show you care about them and they will likely reciprocate.

More importantly, when you write several notes a day to your contacts, you will start being viewed in a different light. By being viewed as a caring and concerned connection, you remove thoughts by others you are out to gain something or have a hidden agenda.

If you practice the steps and techniques in this book, you will see a noticeable difference in your business in 90 days. You will see full benefits within six months.

You will see the way we do business is changing and you will understand how important it is to stay ahead of the curve and be in a position to profit.

Tips for Improving Success

The best way to Position Yourself for maximum results is to create the conditions inviting success.

The examples of return on investment described here are representative, not unique. People in all walks of life, in varied professions and from diverse backgrounds have similar examples in their files. Of course, some have more and better examples than others.

One reason for the difference is certain conditions do encourage quicker and more significant results. There is nothing mysterious about these conditions. The clients who follow all Seven Steps invariably report more substantial and long lasting benefits. Those who seriously neglect one or more steps find their ideas dwindle away. As use of the ideas fades, so do the results. To ensure lasting results, it is best to be attentive to these guidelines:

1. ***Recognize that you cannot achieve your goals by yourself – it takes a network.*** The opportunity for success begins with the understanding that nothing is more important than the people in our lives. There is an old story in networking circles that illustrates this so well. The wife shouts, "The house is on fire!" The husband responds, "Honey, grab the Roladex!"

   Today, it would probably be the database rather than the Roladex. Either way, the concept is the same. The most important asset in our lives is the people with whom we have developed relationships. Understanding this is core to effective networking.

2. ***Believe that effective networking is practical, relevant and beneficial to everyday situations.*** I cannot recall ever meeting someone who had negative comments about personal referrals and networking. The truth is most people do not take it seriously. They have not truly reflected on it as practical, relevant and beneficial to their everyday lives.

People do not resist practical and useful ideas that promise to be supportive of their own best interests. People do resist complicated theories or processes which have no apparent benefits to their lives. People who learn the steps of my Effective Networking Process in a manner enabling them to use the ideas and apply them in real-world situations, will find greater success as they apply them in their lives.

3. ***Commit yourself to applying the Seven Steps properly and regularly.*** To make my Effective Networking Process pay off on a day-to-day basis, there must be a commitment to use it properly and regularly.

While any of the ideas can be used independently, the best results are achieved when all the Seven Steps are used as an integrated process. When the seven steps become a fundamental part of how you conduct business on a daily basis, they reinforce and maximize the effects of each other, resulting in faster and more significant benefits.

4. ***Be creative in how you apply the Seven Steps.*** These steps are flexible and dynamic. People who learn new techniques in a book or classroom are always faced with the question: "But will it work for me?" No matter how great the idea, it remains great, only in theory, until it is used and found workable. That means being able to adapt it to your particular life and your specific situations.

5. ***This process is not something to be implemented in a lock-step fashion.*** It is yours to play with and adapt to meet your needs. As long as you are true to the core concepts and philosophies on which it is based, the playing field is wide open for you to exercise creativity in how you implement the steps and apply them to specific situations in your own life. The more creative you are in tailoring the Seven Steps to fit your life, the more likely you will be to use them and the better the results will be. Give freely, without expecting anything in return. Core to the philosophy underlying my

entire Effective Networking Process is the commitment to giving without the expectation of getting something specific in return. There must be a willingness to give without the expectation of gain.

Anticipation of results is useful only to the extent that it is part of a general belief or faith in the positive power of networking.

On a day to day basis, the focus of the process is to have your eyes and ears open. Listen for other people's needs. Look for gestures you can make such as sending a personal referral, writing a handwritten note, providing advice or serving as a sounding board. These are actions that are at the heart of the process. They are effective because they are offered without wanting something in return. They are the secret to doing business in the relationship age.

6. *Continuously review and assess your efforts, maximize your strengths, fill in gaps and recognize and sharpen your capabilities.* No attempt at something new can be accomplished in a one-time effort. To have lasting and positive effects, your networking efforts must be maintained and fine-tuned regularly. Look for ways to improve your daily habits, strengthen your networks and expand your learning and capabilities. Expand and augment the ideas and their effectiveness will grow with time.

7. *Measure, report and celebrate your successes.* Evaluation of results is vital. Beyond proving how much return is being realized from the investment of your efforts, evaluation of results provides the basis for future decisions about the focus of your networking efforts.

Too often, when success hits, people do not take the time to stop and document it. Feedback of information about successes provides input for future decisions about your networking and marketing efforts and for publicity on your business. Success breeds success. Letting people know about your new clients, new projects and new capabilities will generate interest; resulting in more business. Take time to send a news release to the media, hold a party, write an article or schedule a presentation about a successful project, which came about through networking. Making such results visible does much to enhance success.

8. ***Do not stop; keep going.*** When success comes rolling in, do not stop your networking efforts. Keep watering the garden or you will find that the projects blooming now will soon dry up.

Too often, when people experience great success, they become swept up in the activities that the success brings. Overwhelmed by new business, they justify a temporary halt in their regular networking activities. What was supposed to be a temporary pause becomes more permanent. One day, they find themselves sitting in their office with no current business, no new prospects and a stale database. Do not let this happen to you.

Even when you are experiencing your greatest success, keep working your network. This is the time when you have the greatest chances of leveraging and upgrading the quality of your network by adding new contacts that you find through your successful business.

Effective Networking in the Relationship Age

This book has covered a lot of ground. I hope you will use the concepts to good advantage and return to it from time to time to refresh your memory of the Seven Steps and to spark new ideas.

My Effective Networking Process was developed to help business owners and sales professionals build a solid and lasting referral business. It has gained an impressive track record as a method for bringing people together in ways which result in deep relationships and amazing demonstrations of financial success. People continue to use the Seven Steps because they pay off repeatedly.

As the world moves into a time when personal relationships are increasingly important to doing business, the path to success is changing. Priorities are changing. Lasting relationships which are mutually beneficial take precedence over fast business deals. Personal contacts supersede the impersonal methods of the past.

In this **Relationship Age,** effective networking presides over no miracles. It simply provides a new path for achieving success and forming deep and lasting relationships along the way. As you travel this path, be ready to have your life transformed and, most of all, **Enjoy the Journey!**

ABOUT LARRY KLAPOW

A 19-year Bay Area real estate veteran, Larry Klapow was the President of Coldwell Banker Residential Brokerage's San Francisco Bay Area Region – incorporating 16 offices and a talented team of more than 1,000 real estate professionals.

Prior to being named President in 2007, Larry was the Senior Vice President and Regional Manager of Coldwell Banker Residential Brokerage's San Francisco-Peninsula region, a position that he held from 2001-2007. During his tenure, the San Francisco-Peninsula region's offices earned several outstanding accolades. Most notable was the San Francisco Van Ness office's achievement of number two producing office nationwide. This impressive accolade, combined with countless others, positioned the San Francisco-Peninsula region as one of Coldwell Banker Residential Brokerage's most notable and productive regions in the country.

Prior to serving as Senior Vice President and Regional Manager, Larry was Manager of the company's award-winning Morgan Hill/Gilroy offices. Among Larry's impressive list of managerial accolades: member of the President's Council of Managers (1999-2006) and during his tenure, the Morgan Hill/Gilroy office earned the coveted Premier Office – honoring offices with consistent sales achievement – for four consecutive years. Larry entered real estate in 1990 and was a top producing Sales Associate for seven years before Coldwell Banker Residential Brokerage recruited him to its management team.

Prior to entering real estate, Larry served for 10 years in the United States Navy as a P-3 Orion Flight Engineer.

MANAGED PROFESSIONAL NETWORKS

NETWORKS – SEMINARS – COACHING
RENA PROFESSIONAL NETWORKS INC.

Rena Networks is a professional organization dedicated to helping business owners and sales professionals create a solid and lasting referral based business. We offer exclusive networking teams that meet to create mutually beneficial relationships. Teams are made up of one professional from each major industry. Rena members enjoy lively meetings, mastermind sessions, training and our proprietary technology.

RENA networks also offers:

- Seminars
- Coaching
- Keynotes
- Speaking and training for your event

Contact: Larry Klapow
(408) 710-0796
larry@renanetworks.com
www.renanetworks.com